Lacan Reading Joyce

This book discusses Jacques Lacan's contribution to understanding the life and work of James Joyce, introducing Colette Soler's influential reading to English readers for the first time. Focusing on Lacan's famous Seminar on Joyce, the reader will no doubt learn much from Lacan, but also, as Soler shows, what Lacan learned from Joyce and what perhaps, without him, he would not have approached with so much confidence.

Le Sinthome. This is the title Jacques Lacan chose for his seminar on Joyce in 1975–76. He wrote the word 'sinthome' in its original spelling, from the Greek, and thus used the technique so dear to Joyce: the equivocation between the sound that is heard and the graphic representation that is seen. Is it surprising that the author who recognised in 1956 with 'The Agency of the Letter in the Unconscious' that the Freudian practice of speech revealed an unconscious that writes – something Jacques Derrida found quite remarkable – would end in 1975–76 with Joyce?

Lacan Reading Joyce will be of great interest to professional and academic readers in the respective fields of Lacan and Joyce studies, including psychoanalysts in practice and training, as well as researchers and students in psychoanalytic and modern literary studies.

Colette Soler has been practising and teaching psychoanalysis since 1975, most recently in the context of the School of the Forums of the Lacanian Field (Paris), which she founded. She began analytic training following an encounter with the teaching of Jacques Lacan. Her first areas of study were philosophy and psychopathology, and she has taught both subjects at university level.

The centre for freudian analysis and research library
Series Editors:
Anouchka Grose, Darian Leader, Alan Rowan

CFAR was founded in 1985 with the aim of developing Freudian and Lacanian psychoanalysis in the UK. Lacan's rereading and rethinking of Freud had been neglected in the Anglophone world, despite its important implications for the theory and practice of psychoanalysis. Today, this situation is changing, with a lively culture of training groups, seminars, conferences, and publications.

CFAR offers both introductory and advanced courses in psychoanalysis, as well as a clinical training programme in Lacanian psychoanalysis. It can provide access to Lacanian psychoanalysts working in the UK, and has links with Lacanian groups across the world. The CFAR Library aims to make classic Lacanian texts available in English for the first time, as well as publishing original research in the Lacanian field.

Other titles in the series

The Marks of a Psychoanalysis
by Luis Izcovich

Obsessional Neurosis
edited by Astrid Gessert

Lacan Reading Joyce
by Colette Soler

The Law of the Mother: An Essay on the Sexual Sinthome
by Geneviève Morel

www.cfar.org.uk

https://www.routledge.com/The-Centre-for-Freudian-Analysis-and-Research-Library/book-series/KARNACCFARL

Lacan Reading Joyce

Colette Soler
Translated by Devra Simiu

Lacan, lecteur de Joyce by Colette SOLER
© Presses Universitaires de France

Routledge
Taylor & Francis Group
LONDON AND NEW YORK

First published in English 2018 by Routledge
2 Park Square, Milton Park, Abingdon, Oxon OX14 4RN

and by Routledge
711 Third Avenue, New York, NY 10017

Routledge is an imprint of the Taylor & Francis Group, an informa business

English Edition © 2019 the author Colette Soler

Lacan, lecteur de Joyce by Colette SOLER
© Presses Universitaires de France

Translated by Devra Simiu

The right of Colette Soler to be identified as author of this work has been asserted by her in accordance with sections 77 and 78 of the Copyright, Designs and Patents Act 1988.

All rights reserved. No part of this book may be reprinted or reproduced or utilised in any form or by any electronic, mechanical, or other means, now known or hereafter invented, including photocopying and recording, or in any information storage or retrieval system, without permission in writing from the publishers.

Trademark notice: Product or corporate names may be trademarks or registered trademarks, and are used only for identification and explanation without intent to infringe.

British Library Cataloguing-in-Publication Data
A catalogue record for this book is available from the British Library

Library of Congress Cataloging-in-Publication Data
Names: Soler, Colette, author. | Simiu, Devra, translator.
Title: Lacan reading Joyce / Colette Soler.
　Other titles: Lacan, lecteur de Joyce. English
Description: New York, NY : Routledge, 2018. | "Lacan, lecteur de Joyce by Colette SOLER " Presses Universitaires de France. Translated by Devra Simiu"—Verso title page. | Includes bibliographical references.
Identifiers: LCCN 2018020927 (print) | LCCN 2018031647 (ebook) | ISBN 9780429449352 (Master eBook) | ISBN 9781138327245 (hardback) | ISBN 9781138327252 (pbk.) | ISBN 9780429449352 (ebk)
Subjects: LCSH: Joyce, James, 1882–1941—Criticism and interpretation. | Joyce, James, 1882–1941—Psychology. | Joyce, James, 1882–1941—Influence. | Lacan, Jacques, 1901–1981—Knowledge—Literature. | Psychoanalysis and literature.
Classification: LCC PR6019.O9 (ebook) | LCC PR6019.O9 Z79713 2018 (print) | DDC 823/.912—dc23
LC record available at https://lccn.loc.gov/2018020927

ISBN: 9781138327245 (hbk)
ISBN: 9781138327252 (pbk)
ISBN: 9780429449352 (ebk)

Typeset in Times
by Apex CoVantage, LLC

Contents

	Preamble	vi
1	Introduction	1
2	Symptom, Sinthome	7
3	The Heretic	21
4	An Original Diagnosis	39
5	Symptoms	53
6	Borromean Art	71
7	The Stepladder	91
8	Art-dirp	101
9	Conclusion	111
	Bibliography	127
	Index	129

Preamble

What I am undertaking here is a second reading of Jacques Lacan's contribution to understanding the work and life of James Joyce. The first reading, developed in my course at the Clinical College of the Lacanian Field in Paris, was presented in *L'Aventure littéraire, ou la psychose inspirée: Rousseau, Joyce, Pesoa* (Éditions du Champ lacanien, 2001).

With a distance of fifteen years, this second reading, which follows my re-reading of Joyce's work and of the conceptual revisions introduced by Lacan in the 1970s, completes the first reading, corrects various points, but above all aims to point out something new: what Lacan learned from Joyce and what perhaps, without him, he would not have approached with so much confidence.

Chapter 1

Introduction

The Sinthome. This is the title Jacques Lacan chose for his seminar devoted to Joyce in 1975–1976. He wrote the word 'symptom' in its ancient spelling, coming from the Greek, thus introducing what Joyce made use of: the equivocation between the sound that is heard and the graphic representation that is seen. Is it surprising that the author who began in 1956 with 'The agency of the letter in the unconscious', a text in which he recognised that the Freudian practice of speech revealed an unconscious that writes – something Jacques Derrida found quite remarkable – would end in 1975/1976 with Joyce?

The literary stake is certain and Lacan does not recoil from formulating his hypothesis about the writing of Joyce, new master of the unreadable: he put an end, Lacan said, to the dream of literature (J/L, p. 36). This is a double thesis, about literature, as distinct from poetry, and about Joyce. Dream! This term provides sufficient indication that the literary stake is being measured against the yardstick of psychoanalysis. This is not a paradox, given that literature and psychoanalysis both share the same question: how far can one go, what can one obtain, with the word as sole instrument, be it spoken or written? I use the term 'psychoanalysis', but this means psychoanalysis in the Freudian tradition, where Lacan wished to open a new path, in both theory and in practice, going from the romance of free association to the real of what does not speak: the letter.

This is where he encounters Joyce. More precisely, this is where he encounters Joyce for the first time as a question for psychoanalysis, because he had encountered his work many years before. We know that in his youth, Lacan had frequented Adrienne Monnier's bookshop, Shakespeare and Company, and there heard readings from *Ulysses*. We cannot ignore the fact that Lacan had a thesis about Joyce as early as 1967, in his text 'La méprise du sujet supposé savoir', well before *The Sinthome*. But when he came back to him, in the period of the Borromean knot, his questions were completely different. Interestingly, Lacan did not make use of Joyce the way a so-called 'man of letters' would. On the contrary, he recognised in him the writer [*l'écrivain*] – let me say, not in vain [*pas vain*] – who, in the literary field, had paradoxically brought about a passage toward the real of the letter, beyond its effects of meaning. Now, according to the Seminar of the year before, *R.S.I.* (Real, Symbolic, Imaginary), this is precisely what the symptom does, the symptom that is of interest to psychoanalysis: it makes the unconscious exist in the real, the real of *jouissance*. It is from this standpoint that Lacan reads Joyce. There is thus a clear convergence. The thesis is complex and deserves to be made explicit, but it shows that the question is far from being only literary.

Lacan was truly seized by Joyce – I think this is a good way to put it. He returned to him as if by chance (*tuché* in Greek) when, at the insistence of Jacques Aubert, he attended the James Joyce International Symposium, held in Paris on 16–20 June 1975. But really there is no question that, already for several years, he had been as if . . . inhabited. Lacan's published writings attest to this. So do the many allusions made in passing, for example, in the '*Postface*' to *Seminar XI* in 1973 (Lacan, 2012), and at the end of the lecture on '*The Symptom*' (4 October 1975), so before the seminar and yet again in the '*Preface to the English-language edition of Seminar XI*' (18 May 1976). There are others. But if he was seized, it was to dig deeper the furrow he had opened in psychoanalysis, the furrow of the real at stake in it. In 1975, this problem was nothing new for Lacan, nor was the question of the function of writing for the unconscious, which Freud's practice had shown to be 'structured like a language' to be deciphered in speech. But in 1975 he posed the problem in new terms, linked to his thesis of the real unconscious and the function of the Borromean knot, introduced a few years earlier. Lacan attempted to rethink the whole of the analytic experience with his new schema, including the classical diagnostic categories of neurosis, psychosis, and perversion, and above all, the possibility of a terminable analysis. As we know, the question began with Freud and it is warranted, for Freudian practice – defined as it is by language structured solely as free association under transference and the deciphering of the unconscious – has no principle for ending, any more than does the series of whole numbers with which one can continue to count all the way to infinity. How then to situate an ending – and the nature of the changes produced in the desire and symptoms of the analysand – without convoking what is not language, the real?

Thus, in *The Sinthome*, the seminar dedicated to Joyce, there are several things at stake. I will not take up all of them, only those that determine the reading Jacques Lacan made of James Joyce, together with their impact on the progress of his own advances. There is, first of all, Lacan's interrogation, as an analyst, of the case of James Joyce, his person and his place in the new categories of the Borromean clinic. Here we should not forget that it was Joyce who had offered himself as a case, that of 'the artist', with a definite article, in *Portrait of the Artist as a Young Man*.

Parallel to this, there inevitably arises another question about the function of the written work, in terms of its possibility and even its possible necessity, for its author. The analyst doesn't need Joyce to be concerned with this question. It arises each time someone asks for an analysis to help with 'writer's block'. Moreover, the writer who struggles to put pen to paper has become an important theme in literature. And hence the question of the written work in an author's subjective economy.

Well before Joyce, St Thomas – so important to the young Stephen Dedalus (Joyce, that is) – at the end of a lifetime of writing devoted to nothing less than a . . . *Summa* – described as *sicut palea*' the function of the work as object, equating it to a waste object, to put it politely. This is the function of destitution of the subject, the very same function that awaits the analysand at the end of an analysis, according to the 'Proposition on the analyst of the School' (Lacan, 1968). Was this the case for Joyce, or was it the opposite, an instance of the unanalysable? This, in a nutshell, is the problem.

And where did he get his artistic know-how? An altogether different question, the question of 'know-how' that comes up more than once in the Seminar. Although not elaborated at length, Lacan throws a rather original light on this question. I have no doubt that it conceals another implicit question about the know-how that the act of the analyst supposes. Lacan credits the analyst with a knowledge. He spoke about this for an entire year (1975) at Sainte-Anne Hospital, the very heart of the psychiatric institution, under the title 'The knowledge of the psychoanalyst', undoubtedly in response to the theme of 'non-knowledge' in vogue at the time, especially among members of his School, which he described as a 'mystagogy of non-knowledge' (Aé, p. 359). Know-how is something altogether different, and the question is of great consequence. Generally little inclined to grant absolution, Lacan said: 'One is only responsible within the limits of one's savoir-faire' (S, p. 47).

But certainly more far reaching is the problem of the end of analysis which, I have said before, is bound up with the question of knowing whether or not it can assure a passage to the real that would put an end to the wild imaginings (lucubrations) of the transference, limit the dimension of meaning, and wake one up from the waking dream that speaking beings inhabit.

And that does not even take into account what is at stake with the Borromean knot . . .

It is not surprising, then, that the style of the Seminar borrows nothing from the style of the Joyceans so attached to each word, so concerned with each detail, so devoted to elucidating each point and tracing each of Joyce's allusions. On the contrary, in *The Sinthome*, there is no fascination whatsoever with the text of the author who is his object; nor will one find anything that resembles a proper literary analysis. Lacan obviously evokes the text in passing, comments on some epiphany, some expression or some contribution to the vast literature about Joyce. But even so, he says very little about it, even though he has read Joyce carefully and examined the critics who are legion. The page he devoted in his Seminar to one Mark Shechner, who believed he had analysed *Ulysses*, speaks volumes. This analysis, Lacan says, 'makes a terrifying impression' (S, p. 56). Immediately afterwards, he feels obliged to makes excuses for some of Freud's inclinations in a similar direction. As for the Joyceans, he summarises their work as 'consisting in wondering why Joyce put such and such thing here or there. Naturally, they always find a reason why; he put it there because, just after, there is another word' (p. 132). As for Lacan, apart from his demonstrations and explications of various Borromean knots, which I will not go into, he pushes forward with many questions, questions that will await answers over the course of several sessions, such as: was Joyce mad? Indeed, this is a question that he specifically asks. Recalling Picasso's formula 'I do not seek, I find' (p. 74), Lacan notes that it does not apply here for, in fact, he is seeking. But, conversely, the Seminar makes a number of categorical assertions that form a thesis, most of them awaiting argumentation. An example – I will take it up later – is his discussion of the woman he eventually names as Nora Joyce.

Often enough psychoanalysts speak of deferring to the artist. Lacan himself did this with Marguerite Duras, and more generally when he said that one should 'take a leaf from the book' of artists. But this was before Joyce; with him it was something different. It is not his text that he admires. He does not hide the fact that, as for the poems, he finds them unconvincing; and as for *Finnegans Wake*, he agrees with a critic who finds it tiresome. And Lacan makes clear the reason why: because it neither arouses our sympathy nor causes anything to resonate with our unconscious. This poses the unavoidable question: why read it?

But if Lacan, analyst, does not admire the writer, he does admire the case, and more precisely what Joyce, thanks to his art, managed to do with his life and the conditions of his birth. This is truly what allows him to be called 'Joyce, the symptom' (J/L, pp. 21 and 31).

We know how much Freud looked to literature but, as far as he was concerned, it was in artists that he recognised the precursors of psychoanalysis and in literary texts the opportunity to put the analytic method to the test. From Sophocles to Goethe, from Jensen to Dostoevsky, he thought of literary fiction as anticipating the discovery of the unconscious; the writer's elaboration was homologous to that of the analysand who attempts to speak his truth – to be interpreted, although it can only be half-said. Thus when the neurotic recounts his family history – which he never fails to do in his analysis – this is likened to telling a story. And if Freud speaks of the neurotic's 'family romance', it is to say that the scenario for this story has the structure of a novel. The artist's know-how is conceived as the equivalent of what he himself called the 'work of the unconscious', an unconscious that speaks, an unconscious that constructs messages that need to be deciphered. By putting literary works on the same level as the series of formations his practice interprets – the dream, the lapsus, the bungled action, the message of the symptom – he has not exactly avoided the pitfall of applied psychoanalysis.

On this point, Lacan reversed the Freudian perspective: analytic interpretation does not apply in literature. Every attempt in this direction has always been futile and totally incapable of serving as the basis for any literary judgment. For any work, whether it be poetry or a novel, the text can always be interpreted, that is to say, we can give it meaning. Here psychoanalysis verges on being a hermeneutics. But this meaning has nothing to do with the work itself. Indeed, as I have said elsewhere (Soler, 2001), one possible definition of the work in its relationship to meaning is to say that it resists interpretation as much as it leads to it, remaining always open to the revised readings that are the delight of literary criticism, while at the same time existing outside those readings. Between its meaning and its existence, there is no common measure. The enigma remains on the side of production, forever attached to a know-how that is not subject to interpretation. I could pastiche Lacan in saying: 'that one writes remains forgotten behind what one writes'.[1] In other words, when works are read as a message, these readings say nothing about the activation of the know-how which produced it or had effects. 'Joyce the Symptom' is not an interpretation of the Joycean work. It is an original diagnosis of what Lacan called, as did Joyce himself, 'the artificer'. A diagnosis of uniqueness, therefore, and contrary to any standard: a diagnosis of 'absolute difference' (Lacan, 1998a, p. 276), the only diagnosis worthy of a psychoanalyst.

In the Seminar devoted to Joyce, the reader no doubt learns much from Lacan, but I propose to examine something else: what Lacan learned from his reading of Joyce.

Note

1 Speaking about analysis, in *L'étourdit* Lacan said: 'that one says is forgotten behind what is said in what is heard' (1973, p. 5) making the distinction between what is said, the truth of the saying, its meaning and the act of saying itself.

Chapter 2

Symptom, Sinthome

It is not easy to approach the seminar on *Joyce le symptôme* without some preliminary remarks, given that Lacan reads Joyce on the basis of his elaborations of the time. Take, for example, the term 'symptom', to which he had given a new definition the previous year in *R.S.I.* The use of the term was reworked to such an extent that he changed its meaning.

First, I will put this into perspective in relation to Freud. We know that Lacan returned to Freud, in opposition to the analysts of his time. He claimed to be a follower of Freud, indeed, an authorised follower. But he also deviated from him; and he significantly corrected him. In particular, this happened with the Oedipus complex, which he recognised but also very swiftly and sometimes very virulently criticised. He objected to it not with the mirror of an anti-Oedipus but with a 'beyond Oedipus', the first figure being, we must not forget... the woman, insofar as she is 'not all' in the Oedipus complex (Soler, 2003a, pp. 17–18).

Freud's novel

In the beginning of psychoanalysis was 'Freud's novel' (Aé, p. 309). I will put it this way. Now, what does a novel do but tell a story. Freud paid attention to those told by his analysands. For everyone, the dream tells a story, sometimes a very bizarre one. But there is also our waking dream, the one Freud called 'the neurotic's family romance'. It is always the story of an unhappy childhood in which the most burning desires are unfulfilled. It haunts the subjectivities of adults who most often remain the child they were (Soler, 2013), such that we can speak of the 'ubiquitous child' (Aé, p. 369). At the heart of this memorialised, at times mythicised story, of which everyone bears the traces, Freud, through deciphering symptoms, recognised the presence of an unknown kernel, the fixity of a scenario that dwells within each speaking being, expressed in each of his utterances, in all of his acts. Yet the subject knows nothing about it until an analyst eventually reveals it to him. According to Freud, it is called the phantasy. Lacan said: fundamental phantasy. A story within a story, an invariant of historical memory that anchors the dialectical slippage of meaning. Let us call the phantasy a 'one-way street', sustaining desire, regulating all relations between a subject and others, and between a subject and the Other of discourse. A 'one-way street', but one that goes around in circles, like a story told by the stand-up comic Raymond Devos. And Freud asserts that, for each of us, in the end there is just one indestructible unconscious desire, to be interpreted, particularly in dreams. But curiously, he adds that a single dream, completely interpreted, could alone yield the meaning that orients an entire life. Lacan could call this phantasy novel real in his Seminar *La logique du fantasme*. Its constancy removes it from the dialectic of linguistic narrative and, by virtue of this fact, puts it in the position of an invariable postulate, an anchoring point for all the stories that each of us tells about ourselves, about our own lives.

And we certainly tell stories! We tell them to children, big and small: fairy stories, horror stories, stories about the Santa Claus who doesn't exist. We know the emotion when a child confirms Santa's non-existence: rage at having been fooled by his parents' lies, refusal to believe it, the regret for a lost dream; and sometimes a child who pretends to believe, to spare the feelings of parents who need to believe he still believes. The catch is that, for everyone who speaks, every story lies about the real, from which he or she is separated by the imaginary and the symbolic. At best, stories tell some truths, '*varités*', as Lacan called them, condensing 'variety' and 'verity'. But *the truth* lies, it has the structure of a fiction. It is a lie without a liar, a destiny prepared for us by the imaginary and the symbolic, insofar as they are separated from the real, which is outside the symbolic, outside meaning. Thus, we resort to the 'not real' truth that is articulated in the structure of language, and we do this precisely to fend off our anguish of the real.

We can confirm this today in current affairs. The more the results of science produce anguishing 'advents of the real', – be they in economics, biology, or the military, part and parcel of the capitalistic organisation of the world – the more we appeal to stories as antidotes, even stories that frighten, inventing entirely new disasters, leading us to surmise that the worst is what fascinates us. They are barriers to the imminence of real catastrophes. Our epoch pushes stories to the extreme, believing them to be truer. This is an error. Stories lie. This is the case for all them, whether individual, collective, the darkest imaginable, or those beyond imagination, such as the history of our world which, though supported by facts, does not escape the limits of narrative. The contemporary comparison of various historical memoirs would prove this, if proof were needed. This history is precisely what Joyce despised. He saw it as a nightmarish history. Lacan writes '*hystoire*' with a '*y*', as in hysteria, to say it is a forgery, a fiction.

It is interesting to note that, today, we do have doubts about history, we do perceive that it is not science, that it does not reach the real. This is perhaps because, more than any other, the past century has been rudely awakened from its utopian dream by the nightmare, all too real, of an unthinkable exterminating totalitarianism. As for the century just beginning, its unverifiable, so-called 'crises' could teach us a bit about the limits of political vocabulary. This is doubtless why resorting to stories is now at its peak. What are they used for? Some say: to understand the world. A major theme is that citizens – more precisely, voters – lack understanding, so we have to explain things to them. The manufacturing of a good story, a good narrative is referred to as communication. But it doesn't work very well, because everywhere, people suspect a lie; and more importantly, fiction is not what allows us to treat the real.

Freud the theoretician also told a story: his novel of family novels, his catalogue of catalogues which, we know from Bertrand Russell, is not without implying a few logical paradoxes. Freud's novel of novels is his Oedipus story, a fiction of fictions with offspring from Antigone to Hamlet to . . . your 'average' analysand. This romance, told in 'storyettes' is, according to Lacan, the fruit of 'love affairs with truth' (Aé, p. 309), truth that speaks, even if that is all it does. For his story of Oedipus, Freud certainly borrowed from the theatre of antiquity, but only because this was what he believed he heard from the mouths of his hysterics, after having discerned it in his own 'self-analysis'. And it seemed to him to be something eternal. Today, in 2014, how can we not recognise that this evidence is outdated?

Lacan began, ever so politely, by rewriting the Oedipus as his famous paternal metaphor. Next, he called the Oedipus a 'myth', a nobler metaphor than 'romance', for myth aims to articulate a real that the symbolic fails to approach. Here already was a rectification. Finally, in step with his own advances, he at times virulently rejected the Oedipus, in particular in *Seminar X* (*Anxiety*), where he calls it secondary, a delusion, a comedy, of no use in analysis. Lastly, he interpreted it as a symptom. *Totem and Taboo*, he argued, was a symptom produced by Freud's own neurosis. At this point, it fell to Lacan to conceive anew the function of the Father, whose presence in the very experience of our tradition cannot be erased even if today it no longer holds. In fact, he tried to rethink it as a non-Oedipal function: real, a function at once logical and existential. I will come back to this.

This raises a question: does the symptom lie? There was a time when Lacan stated that its cause was truth (É, p. 739). But this is only half-true. He had to add: the symptom comes from the real.

What does not lie

In medicine, a symptom is a sign, the sign of an illness or dysfunction that we seek to mitigate. In common parlance, the symptom belongs to the order of failure. It stops things from working well: an unwelcome anomalous event, imposing itself, from which we want relief. Today, especially in the English-speaking world, there is a willingness to call it a disorder or a problem, stressing its abnormality. From the start, Freud – having inherited the psychiatric classifications of his time – considered symptoms ascribed to 'nervous diseases' as signs of neurosis, signs of the repression of drives that return in painful ways. So, in every case, the symptom, whatever its form, is seen as a problem to solve; and for psychoanalysis, a problem linked to sexuality on account of the implication of the drives. Freud's principal thesis about neurotic symptoms is well known: they are substitutes for sexual jouissance.

A century of psychoanalysis and Lacan's contribution have produced a spectacular reversal, conducive to all sorts of misunderstandings, if one has not followed its construction. In short, what is called a symptom in the clinical sense, the symptom presented to the analyst as something that does not cease imposing itself on the subject, in the form of 'I can't' (e.g. can't stop thinking, can't feel anything in my body, can't act), everything that perturbs relations with others, whether mental or physical, well this troublemaker, this symptom that causes problems for the subject . . . is a solution.

It is a solution to another problem that belongs not to neurosis but to all beings affected by an unconscious that speaks, that is, all human beings. Based on Freud's discovery of the 'the saying of the unconscious' (L'é, p. 10), this has been clear ever since Lacan gave it a formulation: there is no such thing as a sexual relationship, that is, no sexual relationship that can be written with language. Nevertheless, there are drives, the partial drives that Freud described, whose anchoring in the erogenous zones and whose aims are programmed by the operation of saying. For example, to the original Other's saying, to the demand that the mouth open for food, the body responds. This produces an echo through eroticisation of the mouth that, from then on, no food will be able to fill up. This is how the drives are established. Yet, in spite of all the discourse about love, there is no saying to indicate the sexed partner whose body would cause an echo. There is no genital drive, says Lacan, repeating Freud who, starting from 1915 with a footnote to the *Three Essays on The Theory of Sexuality*,[1] emphasised that heterosexuality was a problem that required clarification.

What does 'There is no such thing as a sexual relation' mean? Certainly, there are coupled signifiers in language, signifiers of sex, man and woman; signifiers of generation, father and mother; and also those that construct the corresponding ideals of masculinity and femininity, maternity and paternity. And discourses certainly try to pair these signifiers. But the pairing does not work beyond appearances, beyond a fending-off-being, for these are nothing but semblants that project every manifestation of sexual difference into the register of theatre, indeed of comedy. This does not prevent biologically sexed bodies from entering into bodily contact; it is a fact. It is also a question: what governs the coming together of heterosexual bodies, given that language does not inscribe a pair of signifiers that would correspond to the jouissances derived from sexual coitus but only one, the phallus. This is the supposed scandal of the Freudian discovery! The drives are certainly at play here; they never hesitate regarding the object, be it oral, anal, scopic, or invocatory. But their object is not the sexual partner, only the object that theory designates as 'partial', a part detached from the body: breast, excrement, look, or voice. And at the level of the relationship of bodies, there is no genital drive that designates the object which would respond to the lack of sexual enjoyment of the one who speaks. For 'the jouissance partner (it is understood: sexual) cannot be approached with language'. If, according to Freud, sexual meaning is everywhere, this is because the sexual relation is nowhere. Hence the question of knowing what corrects this deficiency inscribed in structure and makes possible the elective relations that actually exist between sexed beings.

At the end of his teaching, Lacan answers: it is the symptom as product of the unconscious. It plugs the hole of the 'there is no . . .', the deficiency in the sexual relation, with the erection of a 'there is a . . .'. The Other, the standard partner for sexual jouissance, is lacking, but each person's symptom makes up for it. Thanks to language, a singular element is elected which condenses the substitutive jouissance in the relation between bodies. The first consequence imposed by this structure is that there is no subject without a symptom. In the absence of a relation that can be written, there is only the symptom produced by the unconscious that can fix the privileged mode that renders substantial each person's sexual jouissance, even though as a subject he or she is otherwise governed by the great law of lack in being. The symptom is thus a function of exception – a logical function – with respect to the infinite metonymical drift of the partial drives. It anchors and fixes jouissance: '*fixion*', said Lacan, whereas unconscious coding does not cease to displace it within the series of its signs.

For the moment, I am neither justifying nor illustrating this thesis, only stating it. But we can immediately ask how Lacan has moved from Freud's original assertions about the function of the symptom as a 'substitute sexual satisfaction' to the above formulas.

In Freudian terms, the very notions of 'compromise formation' and over-determination make the symptom a masked return of a repressed jouissance. Thus, the symptom is simultaneously real-time jouissance and a linguistic memorial to experiences of the drive. It can be transformed by the work of analytic speech, something Freud demonstrated from the beginning. The unconscious at stake in the Freudian technique of deciphering is indeed 'structured like a language'. From that moment on, we are assured that, far from ignoring it, the logic of language operates in the therapeutic reduction of symptoms. Nevertheless, this reduction allows an irreducible part to remain. We see this very clearly in Freud's famous case of the 'Rat Man': cured of his obsession, he is not only *not* cured of his neurosis, but the rat, this term that condenses jouissance, this term that has been in his unconscious since his youth, is still there. Lacan attempted to account for what in the symptom is untouchable, beyond the possible modifications of what he called its 'formal envelope', that is to say, the envelope of associated signifiers. Regarding the rat in the 'Rat Man', Freud proposed the remarkable series: excrement, money, child, etc. But the rat is irremovable. In fact, from a phenomenological perspective, the fixity of symptoms stands in contrast to the ephemeral formations of the unconscious: the dream, the lapsus, the bungled action, to which we must add the witty remark. It also stands in contrast to what is specific to language, namely the endless metonymical substitution of signs, which is always possible, and which generates meaning.

Is this not because, in the symptom, the signifier is married – if I may put it this way – to something else, something Lacan called jouissance, precisely to distinguish it from simple pleasure, such that the signifier is itself transformed? Jouissance, by investing a term, an element of the unconscious, one of its signifiers, removes it from the chain of deciphering's incessant substitutions. It transforms it into a 'letter', a linguistic element outside meaning – real – that alone is capable of always binding the same being of jouissance. In the symptom, then, the signifier is made letter: the only thing 'to be identical to itself' (*R.S.I.*, 21 January 1975) there where the signifier is always, by virtue of its structure, differential. The letter is therefore the stopping point for the combinatory, and likewise for the shimmering of what at one time Lacan called the 'linguistic crystal'.

Such was the definition of the symptom in *R.S.I.* in January 1975. It stands in contrast to the symptom in 'The Instance of the Letter', where it is defined as metaphor of trauma, that which accounts for the formal envelope by way of the signifying substitution it contains. Such was Lacan's decisive reformulation in his final elaborations on the question of the symptom. Already, it allows us to grasp that when Lacan formulates 'Joyce the symptom', he is referring not to a pathology but to a solution.

As an effect of language, the unconscious objects to the sexual relation and along with it, to the 'there is only the One' and nothing else. But on another level, it produces something that makes up for it: the symptom partner. Experience attests to there being 'no sexual relation'. We have ample evidence that not any woman will suit any man, or vice versa! There is no predetermined formula here. But for each subject, the choice of a partner must satisfy conditions unique to him or her, governed by his or her unconscious. This justifies the expression 'symptom partner', a way of saying that the partner, found by chance or accident, the condition for jouissance, is itself also conditioned by some feature that is unconscious. This is why Lacan can say that, for a man, a woman is a symptom (*R.S.I.*, 21 January 1975). It therefore follows that what used to be called, in classical terms, object choice, is just as analysable as other 'fixions' of symptomatic jouissance such as obsession, conversion, phobia, etc. Freud saw this very clearly. But all of his attempts to account for the singularities of love life involve the Oedipus. From then on, it was a question of knowing precisely what purpose this Oedipal father serves.

Father of the knot

I will start with the most radical foreclosure, the one that is general, due to language, that of the sexual relation, or to use terms Lacan employed from his earliest years: there is no such thing as the genital drive. I have said this before. Yes, there are the partial drives: oral, anal, scopic, invocatory, but no drive that pushes toward the sex act; nothing in the unconscious allows us to think that the sexed being of man and woman are made for each other or for uniting their jouissances. With the Freudian *Eros* came the dream of making one, the aspiration to fusion. But there was a hole in language that Lacan so beautifully called '*troumatisme*', and also 'a central deficiency'. This is why relations between bodies called for an explanation. For Freud himself – while he did not express himself in these terms – it was the symptom we call Oedipal, via identifications to the mother and father, that was supposed to determine the sexual position of each person and to inscribe him within the law. Thus, he postulated that sexual reality depended upon psychic reality.

Years later, making a major theoretical leap, Lacan will finally call this symptom a '*père-version*', the father version of the symptom: a father whose desire and saying inscribe a model of relationship to a woman that compensates for the sexual non-relation (R.S.I., ibid.). It is an example of a specific regulation of relations between the sexes and the generations, in which a heterosexual couple, a man and a woman, take responsibility for their descendants.

It was in 1975, in *R.S.I.*, that Lacan explicitly formulated the thesis that the Father is a symptom. Cleary, this supposed the prior formulation of 'no such thing as a sexual relation'. For it was this defect that made it possible to understand the paternal mode of jouissance as a supplementation symptom, as he put it in the seminar just quoted. What is less apparent is that the thesis also rests on a prior formulation of the function of saying in sexuation, which Lacan had articulated in 1972 in *L'étourdit*. I will not go into the complexity of the thesis except to note that Lacan joins two dimensions – jouissance and saying – in the notion of sinthome, introduced in relation to Joyce just after *R.S.I.* and in the opening sentences of *The Sinthome*. After some trial and error, Lacan defines '*sinthome*' as the saying that allows the knotting of the three consistencies, symbolic, imaginary and real; and the father is a *sinthome* inasmuch as – by his saying – he names, in particular, his offspring. Lacan says: 'paternal care'. If the father is thus not only a kind of jouissance symptom but also a *saying sinthome*, he operates at the same time at levels other than sex, and notably at the level of a certain transmission.

All of this was implied in the Oedipal metaphor, which was supposed to allow a subject to establish, thanks to the signifier of the phallus, the first layer of his identificatory position and resolve what Lacan called the 'enigma' both of his 'ineffable and stupid existence' and of his 'living being' (É, p. 459) by inscribing it in a lineage of desires, however reductive that might be. Plainly, one cannot disregard the fact that this model of regulation, in addition to being too readily equated with the structure of the conjugal family, is also questioned in our contemporary culture.

It also left questions regarding how a subject, lacking such regulation, could establish his identity; and what sort of partner could work for him or even sustain him. Clinically, one can see this problematic and the delusional response to it in the case of Schreber. Lacan took it up again in his essay 'On a Question Prior to Any Possible Treatment of Psychosis' (É, pp. 445–88) well before the formulations of 1975.

Beyond the paternal metaphor, with the thesis of the symptom partner and the father as supplementation symptom, we come to realise that the generalised foreclosure of the relation between the sexes can either be compensated for via the classical path of *'père-version'* ('turning to the father') or, on the contrary, intensified by the effects of the deficiency of the *symptome-père* ('father-symptom'). That is unless – a third possibility – a supplementation symptom is introduced.

If I insist on the order of Lacan's propositions, it is because their sequence is inseparable from their intelligibility. It is not rare for genuine advances to occur within a *work in progress*, as happened with Lacan. But what is unique about it, indeed what makes it difficult, comes from an apparent absence of didactic concern, at least at that particular time of his teaching, which is all the more curious given how different this is from his repeated appeals to his audience for their responses, notably during the year of *The Sinthome*. Now, from the 1970s on, the question became even more complex with the new schematic of the Borromean knot, including the demonstrations and commentaries Lacan devoted to it. It was up to the reader to follow the thread or threads – never highlighted, often tangled – of a text that was a mix of assertions, ellipses, questions, arguments, repetitions, emphases: its enunciation, without reaching the level of enigma, called out for explanation. Lacan himself, in the 'Overture' to the *Écrits*, said he wanted 'to lead the reader to a consequence in which he must pay the price with elbow grease' (É, p. 5). To say the least!

We must not lose sight of the fact that Lacan made use of the ancient spelling of symptom – sinthome – in relation to Joyce, even though, in the preceding seminar (*R.S.I.*), the emphasis had been on 'the father who names'. I will therefore review, in very general terms, Lacan's successive steps toward this very distinctive diagnosis: Joyce the symptom.

Sinthome is the first word of the first seminar devoted to James Joyce, on 18 November, 1975. However, in the lecture published four years later in 1979 and seemingly written after the seminar, Lacan begins by saying 'Joyce the symptom'. Those who were paying attention could hear him alternate between the two locutions throughout the seminar. Hence the question: are they one and the same, in which case one could choose one or the other, or do the two spellings correspond to two definitions, and hence two different functions? The question might seem abstract but what is at stake is hardly that: it is nothing less than what, from time to time in *R.S.I.*, Lacan called the real subject, not simply the supposed subject of the signifier, but the subject who has an enjoying body, and for whom the possibility of a social link is posed. Today these links appear so precarious that the question of 'living together' is omnipresent.

Lacan first approached the question in his construction of the 'Four Discourses', where he attempted to situate it on the basis of the Borromean knot. The problem is that jouissance in itself is not binding; on the contrary, it is bound to *Thanatos*. Freud noted this. The one who has no law other than his own *fixion* of symptomatic jouissance can remain outside the social link. Hence the question of the possible knotting of, on the one hand, 'the jouissance proper to the symptom . . . the opaque jouissance that excludes meaning . . .'. (J/L, p. 36), a real disconnected from the imaginary, to which Joyce attested with many of his traits; and on the other hand, meaning, produced between the Imaginary and the Symbolic, to which psychoanalysis resorts in order to 'fix' what in the symptom is outside meaning. With the Borromean knot, the question is thus posed of knowing how, under what conditions, and with what effects, these three dimensions can hold together. And if it is the *sinthome saying* that knots them, one cannot avoid distinguishing the symptom from the jouissance that is outside meaning.

By the end of *R.S.I.*, Lacan had concluded that the knotting of three – Real, Symbolic, and Imaginary – supposed a fourth, precisely what, the following year, he would call the *sinthome*. What is this? Once again, I will spare the details and get straight to the point: it is the *dit-mension* of saying, specifically, of the saying that names. From this comes the idea of the *Père-sinthome (Father-sinthome)*, which is not to say that it occurs only in the Father. Thus, when the knot is tied, it is as if each of these three dimensions is under the jurisdiction of the others. The *dit-mension* of meaning, produced between Symbolic and Imaginary and so essential to those who speak, finds itself knotted to the Real which by definition is outside meaning. In addition, meaning is limited by the Real. If this were not the case, the free association utilised by psychoanalysis would be too free to be fruitful.

Clinically, Lacan started from an emphasis on 'elementary phenomena', having entered psychoanalysis by way of the study of psychosis, with his *Aimée* case (Lacan, 1975a). At the time, he did not speak in terms of unknotting, but in terms of ruptures in the chain of speech and language, or the failure of 'quilting points'. He established these as the hallmarks of psychosis, as the effect of the foreclosure of the Name-of-the-Father. These range from hallucinations to the 'as if' conformism of holophrastic discourse, from interrupted phrases to manic logorrhoea. All of these are manifestations of what he had already called the signifier in the real: in other words, outside the chain. Correlatively, one also finds what I can call a liberation of meaning which, the moment it is freed from the chain of language, surges everywhere, with the most neutral of realities given meaning in delusional interpretation. Proof by its opposite of the necessity of knotting.

This means that the free association of which psychoanalysis makes use is not free at all, something that every analysand is aware of. It bears fruit only because it turns round and round in the circle of the phantasy, where symbolic articulation, imaginary scenarios, and the real of jouissance are knotted. The efficacy of free association is thus conditioned by the *sinthome* that knots and, if the Father is a kind of *saying sinthome* that knots, we can say that psychoanalysis relies on the *father sinthome*, 'dupe of the father' *(J/L*, p. 36). This has nothing to do with the little story of Oedipus, to which I will return. It is important to see how jouissance is involved in the knot of the three consistencies. All jouissance is configured by the 'apparatus' of language (Lacan, 1999, p. 22), but the knot houses distinct jouissances: phallic jouissance, '*joui-sens*', and jouissance of the symbol-letter are all found there together. Lacan wrote the term *joui-sens* for the first time in *Television*, in 1973, but he had been working on this idea since his definition of the symptom as a metaphor of trauma (É, p. 431). The three cases concern the 'way in which each one enjoys his or her unconscious' (*R.S.I.*, 18 February 1975). Thus, the modality of jouissance will differ in accordance with whether or not there will be a knotting sinthome. When a knot is made, the metabolism of jouissance is Borromean; the three jouissances hold together. In the absence of a knot, the jouissance of letters outside meaning, between Symbolic and Real, and the *joui-sens* of language, between Symbolic and Imaginary, can play their parts separately (Soler, 2014). The result will be either the illness of the Real – the jouissance of the Symbolic real-ised by the letter, ignoring all other partners, foreclosing truth – or, contrary to this, the 'illness of mentality', as Lacan diagnosed it, the illness of meaning that floats free in the Imaginary, without a body, unhooked from the Real.

The path of saying

Lacan took some time – indeed all of *R.S.I.* (as I pointed out in my seminar *La querelle des diagnostiques*, 2003–2004) – to make of the *sinthome* a saying, specifically a saying that names, and even another name for the one who names. The result: there can be *sinthomes* other than the *Father-sinthome*, because the *sinthome* is itself father of the name. The time it took Lacan to come to this conclusion had to do not so much with acknowledging the necessity of a fourth term, but with recognising a saying which is not necessarily that of the Oedipal father. In *R.S.I.*, he said: 'For three to be knotted, is there a requirement for the *plus one* to have a consistency that is referred to the function of the Father? The Borromean knot demonstrates the contrary' (*R.S.I.*, 11 February 1975). And, in his interrupted seminar *Les non-dupes errent*, he added that with the use of the plural, he already had the idea of a possible *supplementation* to the paternal saying, as a fourth Borromean consistency. The proof is in Joyce, whose renaming of himself rivals the Borromean Father. I will come back to this.

Lacan says: 'We specify the saying as what makes the knot' (ibid.), whereas the word slips. On the level of practical manipulation or material fabrication of a Borromean knot, it is possible to have a Borromean knotting with only three circles or three squares, provided the shapes are closed, even in the form of an infinite straight line. But on a clinical level, the *saying fourth* is indisputably required. Indeed, in psychoanalysis, the Borromean knot is called upon to account for the effects of an experience of speech; and since speech has to be uttered, there must have been a saying. The 'spoken knowledge' of the unconscious certainly comes from *lalangue*, but this presupposes there has been a saying of this *lalangue*. Indeed, when I state that, at the level of the material creation of the Borromean knot, a knot of three is possible, this is not false. But 'one has to do it', as Lacan says, and this is not simply a truism. The knot is made for the 'speaking being' (*parlêtre*) by saying; for strings, it is made by doing. To better understand knots that are constructed on the basis of saying, Lacan chose the path of exploring Borromean knots and chains that one can actually make with one's hands, and also draw.

I hardly think that Joyce whispered in Lacan's ear about the function of saying! On the contrary, since *L'étourdit* (1973), Lacan had it at his disposal; this is why he could propose an interpretation of Joyce's specificity. But saying is not to be confused with the voice. 'Saying is an act' (*R.S.I.*, 18 May 1975). It is existential, an emergence, sometimes an absolute choice. In the beginning was the saying, from this Lacan moves to the *dieure. S*aying produces *dieure*, the creator. One must rewrite the catechism. What is God? God is saying; speech presupposes saying and only comes second. The signifier is, of course, *ex nihilo*, and poses the problem of existence since one can always talk about what does not exist. Yet is must be uttered, and it is the saying that testifies to existence. 'Let there be light'. This is the text, but to go from there to 'and there was light', required its saying. To put it differently, in the knot of three, the saying 'remains forgotten' (Aé, p. 449). It is the fourth that invisibly holds the three consistencies born by speech. But saying is not speech. It is, according to Lacan, its 'emission' and also its 'ejaculation'. Without saying, there are no 'saids' by which the three can be knotted. It is common to say, 'never two without three'. With knots, there are never three without four, three being the minimum, just as three in a series of whole numbers presupposes a fourth, according to Frege, who was able to show that, in the series of numbers, the zero is an unconditional element.

Hence, for the analysand, what has been done or not done by the primordial saying can be undone or redone by the analytic saying. A child is first of all a body, the product of two organisms, the reproduction of bodies, even when copulation of sperm and egg occurs outside the body. But the speaking being – he or she – is an effect of *lalangue* on the body only because he or she is the child of the family saying, or rather of the way in which he or she has received this saying, coming as it does from a pair of speeches, those of the couple, whether discordant or not. Here we need to correct the bias of certain readings of the *Geneva Lecture* which, in stressing exclusively the impact of *lalangue* on bodies, forgot that the function of the maternal *lalangue* itself depends on the act of saying, on the way in which this saying has mobilised *lalangue* into a discourse, in which the child will read how he or she has been received, as Lacan says. In other words, he or she will read the desire that has welcomed him beyond just having engendered him. This saying that knots – why not call it *diresir*, to condense '*dire*' (saying) and '*désir*' (desire) – together with the real of *lalangue* and the real of jouissance, is in principle the very same thing Lacan evokes when he speaks of the 'coalescence' of the *motérialité* of the unconscious and of jouissance. Lacan strongly insisted on this in the lectures he delivered at Yale University on 24 November 1975 (Lacan, 1976). Structured language only exists because there is a saying, that is to say, because there are subjects who use *lalangue*. I quote: 'What creates structure is the manner in which, at the beginning, language emerges in the human being' (ibid., p. 444). Now, while there are also bodily conditions, language does not emerge without the saying of people who were there before us, in particular he or she who transmits the maternal *lalangue*, uttered in parallel to the care of the body. The social links, that is, the established discourses, themselves depend on this saying, for the *semblant* functioning as agent in each discourse supposes a saying that hollowed out the place into which that *semblant* enters. More generally, as I have often pointed out, Lacan connects the start of each of the four discourses to a proper name, the name that was the bearer of the saying: Lycurgus, Charlemagne, Freud. Without Freud's saying, there would be no object cause of desire in the place of the *semblant*, and therefore no analytic discourse. A discourse makes a social link, possibly without speech, but not without a foundational saying. Thus, the saying knots not only the three consistencies, but also – at the same time – it knots *parlêtres* to each other. The analytic discourse is a double example of this: one saying has an effect on another saying, that of the analyst on that of the analysand. Another example is the relationship between the generations. There, too, parental saying is the logical condition for all the 'saids' that can mark their descendants. The power to name is itself the power of a saying that inscribes a being in a line of desires, distinct from any material legacy, with no existence other than symbolic. Yet another example comes from politics, where violence is never just raw violence, but violence that has been ordered into a discourse. For each change of discourse, there is a new love, as Lacan says in *Encore*. Indeed, for each change of discourse, there is a new saying that makes a new promise. The power of existential saying is a contingency that is different from that of the traumatic jouissance event of the body. And with this double contingency, well, nothing is guaranteed, all anticipation is thwarted; but on the other hand, nothing is excluded. The field of possibilities is open.

And so it is that the contingency of the *sinthome-saying* has something superior to the pure contingency of jouissance. Indeed, 'the body-event' that is the symptom does not make a social link, involving at most a will to possess another body. But the *sinthome* as saying is not just a body event, even if it does provide jouissance with a Borromean modality. It has another dimension.

Note

1 Freud, S. (1909) Complete Psychological Works of Sigmund Freud, Standard Edition, vol. VII: *Three Essays on the Theory of Sexuality*, 168–9, fn. 3.

Chapter 3

The Heretic[1]

Lacan approached the case and the work of Joyce in terms of the ideas I have just reviewed. To talk about Joyce, he not only revived the old way of writing 'symptom', he also qualified it as 'heretical'. I will start with this. Heretical with respect to which canon? That of the Church fathers? Independent Ireland? Both? Or was it the Freudian Oedipus? If we follow what is developed in the first lesson of *The Sinthome* and in *Joyce le symptôme II*, we see that it is a *heretical sinthome*. The introduction of a new spelling is not some amusing fantasy or piece of erudite coquetry. Instead, it is a conceptual progress. I have studied it closely to grasp what justifies it and to understand its particularity, all the more as, given that in the lecture published in 1979, four years after *The Sinthome*, Lacan opens his argument with 'Joyce the symptom', retaining the conventional spelling.

Lacan tells us that, as a function of the 'two slopes they offered to Joyce's art', he has named his *sinthome with* 'the name he deserves, that suits him, by changing its spelling' (S, p. 7). He then clarifies this further: 'both spellings concern him' (ibid.). This detail shows, at least for that moment, that he did not ascribe the same meaning to 'symptom' correctly spelled. 'Both spellings concern him'. These words are found in the review *Ornicar?* in 1976, in the very first published appearance of *The Sinthome*. They are found again ten years later in *Joyce avec Lacan* edited by Jacques Aubert, where the first two lessons of the seminar appear. But in the 2005 version of the seminar published by Seuil, they have disappeared.[2] All the more reason to examine this, since the omission in 2005 could hardly have been accidental. No doubt, it stemmed from a decision about theory. I can also verify that in stenographies of the seminar, where bias cannot be suspected, the words cut in 2005 are indeed there. Thus we have three versions of the first lessons of *The Sinthome*, all of them edited by Jacques-Alain Miller. Wherever there are differences among the three, my preference is for the texts that appear in *Ornicar?*, published without delay and in sequence, during Lacan's lifetime.

Sinthome, then. A writing rich in equivocations. In French one hears the words '*saint*' (saint) and '*homme*' (man), the '*saint homme*' (saintly man), to whom Lacan dared to compare the psychoanalyst. From there Lacan slides, as always by homophony, to Saint Thomas Aquinas and tells us: 'I put *madaquin* after sinthome, which I spell whatever way you like' (S, p. 6). Sinthome madaquin, then (Saint Tho-mas d'Aquin). Why these verbal games? Well, because from this play with spellings, or rather with misspellings, the multiplicity of equivocations of the sonorous dimension emerge, from which the unconscious – 'spoken knowledge' – is inseparable. However, these plays with writing, in which Lacan pastiches or '*purstiches*' (S, p. 141) Joyce are generally not equal to Joyce, failing to attain the level of polysemy in *Finnegans Wake*. Yet the richness of Lacan's play with writing can evoke not only 'saint' and 'sin' in English, but also '*Sinn*' (sense) in German, and in French 'Saint Thomas' of the *Summa* and – why not – the French word '*somme*' (sleep), from which *Finnegans Wake* is supposed to wake us!

Furthermore, it evokes *Thom's Dictionary*, the Dublin directory of which, according to Jacques Aubert, Joyce made ample use in writing *Ulysses*. But in every case, Lacan's equivocations remain captive to his aim to demonstrate something. For example, when he writes '*LOM*', '*Hessecabeau*', or '*hissecroibeau*', we recognise, in this order: the word '*homme*' ('man'), the 'h' that belongs to '*homme*', the '*esse*' (Latin 'to be') of *être* (French 'to be'), the '*cas beau*' ('beautiful case') or '*le cabot*' (the cur or the ham actor) who elevates himself ('*se hisse*'), believes himself handsome or spruces himself up. The meaning is consistent with his thesis and limits all jouissance to the letter, in contrast to what eventually happens in Joyce, where the letter controls the lightning flashes of possible meaning, that is, meaning reduced to enigma. Similarly, homophony produces the passage from *sinthome* to '*Saint Thomas d'Aquin*', but the sliding does not occur simply through homophony. Indeed, the saint was a champion of what Lacan has called 'the agency of the letter', re-evoked in the first lesson of the seminar. He was also the one who counted most for the young Stephen Dedalus who, according to Lacan, 'really struggled with this saintly man', especially the *claritas*. Indeed, this saint with his *Summa*, had so much to say about divine knowledge, that knowledge that is called for but missed by the signifiers of the subject's half-said truth, would, at the end of his life sign off with his *'sicut palea'*, thus anticipating the *letter/litter*, the letter as waste, reinstated by Joyce.

Another path

The puns Lacan produced following Joyce were all liberties taken with *lalangue*, liberties taken with spelling, but limited by the aims of the saying and always motivated by a reason. For example, take the play between '*y*' and '*i*' in the new writing of symptom. Most of the time, '*Sinthomadaquin*' is transcribed with an '*i*', making it look like – as opposed to sound like – the English word 'sin'. The original sin of jouissance that Thomas Aquinas had worked to reconcile with Aristotle's ethics of moderation. Nevertheless, in a paragraph where what matters for Lacan is the individual specificity of Joyce, Miller (in the *Ornicar?* version) writes it with the '*y*' of symptom: '*synthomadaquin*', the '*y*' he suppresses in subsequent versions. I have no reason to take issue with this '*y*'. It fits with what Lacan argues in that paragraph regarding the question of knowing whether or not Joyce belongs in the canonical line of the good Saint Thomas, in other words, whether or not Joyce was a Saint, to which Lacan replies in the negative. Not only was Joyce not a saint, as Lacan shows in his second lecture, but instead he made the '*madaquinism*' of Saint Thomas fall, by substituting another path. So, the '*y*' inserted in '*synthome*' was useful for marking Joyce's symptomatic specificity.

It is this other path – the path that diverges from Saint Thomas – that Lacan writes as '*sint'home rule*', (S, p. 6) without a '*y*'. Here we have yet another equivocal writing; this time, it takes us to Joyce's heretical *sinthome*. To the French ear, the English word 'rule' evokes something that rolls; Lacan plays with this translinguistic homophony by speaking a little later about the '*symptôme à roulette*'. '*Rule*' is basically what orients government. '*King rule*' refers to government by a king. But writing it as '*sint'home*' with an apostrophe no longer isolates '*homme*' (man) but rather 'home'. 'Home rule': this was the great rallying cry of the demand for Ireland's autonomy and local government. In fact, Joyce gave a lecture entitled 'The Home Rule Comet'. The '*sint'home rule*', the symptom on wheels, this alone commanded him, allowing him both to sustain himself as autonomous and to sustain himself in the world. A *sinthome* of his own, it was not received as a legacy either from his father or from the Church fathers, or even from his fatherland. Far from inscribing him in any order or prior rule, it inscribes his singularity. In sum, a '*sinthome rule*' which does not belong to a saint or to Ireland's 'home rule' which 'made him grind his teeth', according to Lacan. A singular *'sint'home rule'* which made him into a heretic, a double heretic of the Church and of Ireland. What is specific to a heretic is that he is not satisfied with following or receiving. Rather, he chooses. Lacan says: 'It's a fact that Joyce makes a choice', adding that in this regard Joyce is a 'like me, a heretic' (S, p. 7).

So this is the outcome of Lacan's first elaboration with the new spelling: the Joyce-*sinthome* indicates a choice that is heretical. As we shall see, this is a triple choice of heresy: Oedipal, religious, and political.

Indeed, the new spelling of '*sinthome*' with an 'i' was necessary to mark the difference with the usual writing of 'symptom', which designates a modality of jouissance. Jouissance, even if it is jouissance of the letter or letters of the unconscious, *joui-sens*, engages the excitable body. The symptom with a 'y' is far from missing in Joyce, but one could never call it a choice. Quite the opposite: it determines the being of jouissance to the point where it cannot be eradicated; and once fixed, its kernel of the real 'does not stop writing itself'. By contrast, at the level of the *sinthome-saying*, choice is possible, given that saying – if it has effects, no 'saids' without a saying – is not a fact of structure. It is existential, and therefore contingent: an 'event' which has effects on the metabolism of desire and jouissance, but is not structure.

Indeed, in the schema of the three-ringed Borromean knot, where can we put choice? Certainly not on the level of the three consistencies. If the unconscious 'presupposes a knowledge, and a spoken knowledge as such' (p. 112) and if man speaks with his body, this necessarily implies both the Symbolic of signifiers that come from *lalangue* and the Imaginary of body representations, which are joined to each other, but also what resists them both, the Real that is outside meaning. There is no choice here. Choice can only be at the level of knotting, but a fourth consistency is necessary: in its essence, saying, the act of the *sinthome-saying*, existential to such an extent that, in Joyce, the choice can only be called . . . impudent. He wrote: 'Bloom the prudent'. But when it comes to Joyce, it would be more fitting to say: Joyce the impudent.

As Lacan tells us:

> This is where today I'm going to crown what is involved in the Name-of-the-Father, at the very degree to which Joyce bears it out, with what it would be most suitable to call *the sinthome*. It is in so far as the unconscious is knotted to the sinthome, which is what is singular to each individual, that we may say that Joyce, as has been written somewhere, identifies with the individual. He is one who has earned the

privilege [...] of being reduced to a structure that is the very structure of LOM, if you will let me spell it quite simply L.O.M.

(p. 147).

Lom: with these three letters, the writing makes a One. It is essentially the real subject, the one I sometimes call 'Borromean'.

The 'Nego'

It is now a question of knowing where his heretical 'sinthome on rollers' took Joyce (S, p. 6). According to Lacan, heresy is first of all a choice, the choice of a 'path by which to capture the truth' (p. 7). What was the path for Joyce? Just as Lacan said of his art, there were two slopes. Reading his final work, *Finnegans Wake*, one immediately sees that Joyce takes hold of truth by what diffracts it and also by what renders it derisory, namely, by way of the pure letter, outside meaning, paradoxically the opposite of 'the instance of the letter such as it so far has been outlined' (p. 6), as Lacan says. The letter that feeds the symptom of meaning, whose efficacy 'would do no better than to displace the sinthome, even to multiply it' (ibid.).[3] An opposition, then, between the agency of the letter, known since 1955 – that is, the agency of language as carrier of meaning and truth – and the symptom letter which only enjoys. I will come back to this.

For the moment, my focus is on the early works that question truth and, among these, the works said to be autobiographical. The relationship to the Other of discourse is already there and it is remarkable. There is no ambiguity in Joyce's position: he wants nothing to do with it. I have called this position 'negationist' (Soler, 2001) to emphasise the dimension of determination, with its certitude that is almost visceral in its rejection. Joyce himself, in his first version of *A Portrait of the Artist* (1904) speaks of 'his *Nego*'. According to Jacques Aubert, in his Preface to the French edition, '*Nego*' is the first person singular of the performative found in the Latin of the Church. One easily detects the choice here of a performative negation, indeed an active rejection, in the readable passages, by which I mean the passages where James Joyce sought to decipher the enigma of himself: essentially *Stephen Hero* and *A Portrait of the Artist as a Young Man*. Here I will not worry about the gap between the character and the author, nor about the question of the more or less autobiographical nature of the work. The character may well be named Stephen, but how could the supposed subject of the story, of the child's journey through Dublin (as well as the century) be called anything other than James? Is James not

Joyce? Perhaps. Does James not have more than one facet to his portrait? Of course, but one of them is represented here. We can be sure of it, even if we have none of those cross-checks from correspondence or witnesses that allow us to verify biography. For insofar as a text is readable – and these are – it represents a subject, that is to say, a desire and a mode of jouissance. The subject position that develops from 1904 to 1915, in the above-mentioned texts, as well as in works from the same period and in parts of his correspondence, bears the mark of a veritable negative passion – more than a judgment – toward the place of the Other. A paradigmatic example is his relationship to the city of Rome.

Despiser of Rome

It is amusing to think that, but for a few months, Sigmund Freud and James Joyce could have run into each other in Rome. In July 1907, Joyce left; Freud arrived in September. For 'Jim', leaving Rome was the escape from eight trying months in a city he abhorred. For Freud, he had spent an enchanted week in a city that, for him, was always magical.

In July of 1906, Joyce, aged twenty-four, his wife Nora and their one-year-old son, Giorgio, arrived in Rome. It was a half-hearted decision. Two years before, on 8 October 1904, he had fled Ireland with Nora, ending up, via Paris, then Pola, in Trieste to teach at the Berlitz School. After losing this job, he applied for office work at a bank in Rome, a city which he detested immediately, violently. From his letters to his brother Stanislaus, who stayed on in Trieste, we can follow the almost daily development of this strange execration. How bizarre for one suckled by the Jesuits on classical culture, for one absolutely passionate about art, to not love Rome! Such hate at first sight is something rare, perhaps unique in literature, with the exception of Julien Gracq and his Seven Hills. And if Freud admitted that his love of Rome called for interpretation, we can say the same for Joyce's hatred.

When he arrives in Rome on 31 July 1906, nothing pleases him. His reaction is immediate. That day, his first message of six lines ends with 'the Tiber frightens me (too large)!' (SL, p. 90). On 2 August, he writes a bit more, enough to note that 'Romans are excruciatingly well mannered' (ibid.). By 7 August, the balance sheet begins. He has visited St Peter's, the Pincio, the Forum, and the Colosseum. 'S. Peter's did not seem to me much bigger than S. Paul's in London. The dome from inside does not give the same impression of height. S. Peter is buried in the middle of the church'. He expected 'to hear great music [. . .] but it was nothing much. [. . .] The neighbourhood of the Colosseum is like an old cemetery' (SL, p. 91). The merchants, the guides, the young American girls are bothersome. Nevertheless, he admits that the Pincio is a fine garden. Sometime later, on 25 September, he writes: 'I must be a very insensible person. Yesterday I went to see the Forum [. . .] I was so moved that I almost fell asleep . . . Rome reminds me of a man who lives by exhibiting to travellers his grandmother's corpse' (SL, p. 108).

This acrid tone never ceases during the entirety of his stay, rising sometimes to sarcasm, sometimes to hurtful diatribe when it is no longer about 'stupid' monuments but rather about the Italians themselves. On 3 December he wrote: 'I have seen a lot of Romans now and if anyone asks you what I think of them you may say that so far as I can see their chief preoccupation in life is the condition (to judge from their speech) broken, swollen etc of their *coglioni* (testicles) and their chief pastime and joke the breaking of wind rearward' (SL, p. 135). Qualifiers follow: obscene, vulgar, in bad taste, common, puerile, lacking delicacy and virility. Then he regrets having been unnecessarily harsh on poor Ireland, so candid, so hospitable, so beautiful. He ends by finding the Irish to be 'the most civilised people in Europe' (SL, p. 139). On 7 December he writes: 'I hate to think that Italians have ever done anything artistic'. He adds: 'What did they do but illustrate a page or two of the New Testament' (ibid.) How different from Freud's infatuation, finding everything marvellous, from the noise and chaos to the ugliness of the women. In a letter to his family, dated 22 September 1907, Freud writes: 'The women of Rome, strangely enough, are beautiful even when they are ugly, and not many of them are that' (Freud, 1907, p. 261). As for Joyce, he was very soon beside himself: 'I am damnably sick of Italy, Italian and Italians, outrageously, illogically sick' (SL, p. 139).

Illogically? Perhaps not. Affects have their logic.

True, nothing goes well in Joyce's life from the moment he arrives in Rome. He had always believed, with a boundless conviction, in the singularity of his calling as an artist, accepting as obligatory only what he considers due from one whose nature is that of an exception. He mocks those who think 'the duty of man is to pay his debts', proclaims hatred for conventional virtues, warns Nora from the beginning of their relationship that he would never marry her, rejects with his whole soul the idea of domesticity. Now this artist for future centuries finds himself burdened by family and a pencil-pushing job at a bank, sometimes working twelve hours a day, including moonlighting as a teacher. For all that, he is always dramatically out of money. To the boredom and routine of his life as a functionary are added the rebuffs from his publishers, turning his artistic life into nothing but penury and precariousness.

Not a week goes by without urgent requests to Stanislaus to send money, along with instructions on how to borrow it. He counts the number of *lire* he has, the number of days they will be able to feed themselves, what they have eaten and will eat, past and upcoming expenses for rent, clothing, and medicine. What is obvious – but never mentioned in the letters, an open secret well-known to Stanislaus (who is quite fed up with being harassed) – are the incessant nights of drinking, so costly in terms of money, fatigue . . . and recriminations. It is not surprising that he also has to bear Nora's complaints, protests from landlords, and on occasion their eviction notices. One Sunday, entirely spent knocking on doors to find lodging for his (holy) family – to no avail – he compares himself to poor Joseph! In addition, Nora is pregnant again . . .

In a style that is bitter, precise, pseudo-objective, Joyce lays out this life of a galley slave, doubtless making it all the easier for him to beg with a naturalness and sense of entitlement that are remarkable. Indeed, in August 1904, he wrote Nora before the departure from Ireland: 'The actual difficulties of my life are incredible, but I despise them' (SL, p. 26). In the meantime, things – that is, the things that truly matter to him, the fate of his art – have gone from bad to worse: his attempts to publish *Dubliners* have failed (it will be published only in June 1914); he has the idea for *Ulysses* but hasn't written a line, and his creative possibilities seem to him to be in peril.

The previous year, in September 1905, two months after the birth of Giorgio, when he was still living in Trieste, he wrote to Stanislaus: 'My nature is artistic and I cannot be happy so long as I try to stifle it [. . .] I have a habit [. . .] of following up a conviction by an act. If I once convince myself that this kind of life is suicidal to my soul, I will make everything and everybody stand out of my way as I did before now' (SL, p. 74). In December 1905, he tells his Aunt Josephine that he is considering leaving Nora. On 18 October 1906, the question is still there: '[Is it] possible for me to combine exercise of my art with a reasonably happy life?' (SL, p. 121). Then, on 14 February, without warning, he will inform Stanislaus of his sudden resignation from the bank. He admits he did a *'coglioneria'* but really he does not believe it, since immediately he adds: 'I fear that my spiritual barque is on the rocks. has run aground. There is some element of sanity in this last mad performance of mine, I am sure' (SL, p. 150).

From here it would be easy to think that Joyce's rejection of Rome was nothing but an effect of his bad mood, a space of abreaction for his internal contradictions. Richard Ellmann (1982), his principal biographer, is not far from this hypothesis. He goes so far as to mention 'depression' and notes that, in this period, Joyce expresses an almost systematic revulsion for everything, especially for whatever English literature he happens to be reading. It is true that at the end of his stay Joyce is hurting from the rejections of his publishers, upset at not taking part in the Dublin theatrical debates, exasperated with Nora's recriminations, frightened by her new pregnancy. For all that, Joyce could just as well have hated Trieste where, objectively speaking, his fate was not much better except for – it is true – his work. He finds Rome 'more dissipating than dissipation' (SL, p. 141) and affirms that he wants none of it. Nevertheless, we know for a fact that his vituperations against 'the stupidest old whore of a town ever I was in' (p. 135) took place long before the days of pencil pushing and successive disappointments. Nor is this some posing by an author. Joyce is truly affected by Rome, to the point of having nightmares. Fifteen days after his arrival he writes: 'I am troubled every night by horrible and terrifying dreams: death, corpses, assassinations' (p. 96). To evoke the shadow of death would be to say too little. Doubtless, the contingencies of his life provide the context but not the foundation for his immediate rejection of Rome, followed by continuous vituperations. No, there is something more viscerally intimate to this virulence. It has to do with his being.

Freud's love of Rome is equally consistent with what we know of him. It is no surprise that this explorer of the subjective past, so curious about earlier civilisations, collector of antiquities, was enchanted by a city where things began. But if Joyce's execration is like the negative face of Freud's exalted enthusiasm, would a reverse interpretation not then be possible?

With Freud, he makes the interpretation himself. In spite of his discretion and elliptical style in deciphering his own case, several remarks from his correspondence – where he speaks of the internal obstacle opposing his Rome voyage, the subjective effect of resolving this impediment, the euphoria that this city always inspired in him and, above all, his reference to Hannibal – leave no doubt: one understands that *mutatis mutandis*, his interpretation of *A Disturbance of Memory on the Acropolis* (1936) as the son's desire for transgression, applies just as well to Rome. For Joyce, must we, once more, make use of the *ready-made* interpretation by way of the father?

It would be easy to justify. For example, on 29 August 1904, Joyce confessed to Nora that, six years earlier, he 'left the Catholic Church, hating it most fervently. [. . .] Now I make open war upon it by what I write and say and do' (p. 48). How, then, could he love the city of our Holy Father?

He does admit that ancient Rome must have been beautiful. It is rather 'Papal Rome' he denigrates and lowers to the level of 'any secondary quarter of a fine metropolis' (SL, p. 115). About the Pope, he describes how, on 13 November, with a few minutes to himself, he goes to the Vittorio Emanuel Library, where he finds time to read the report on the 1870 Vatican Council, which had declared the infallibility of the Pope. He summarised it thus: 'The Pope said: "Is that all right, gents?". All the gents said "Placet" but two said "Non placet". But the Pope "You be damned! Kissmearse! I'm infallible!"' (SL, p. 190).

In brief, it would make a nice thesis to say that Rome inherited the relationship of the son to the Father: for Freud, a respectful emulation which makes the son excel, for Joyce an insolent rejection which 'sends packing (*verwerfe*) the whale of an imposture' (É, p. 484). Let us not forget the extent to which Bloom embodies derision of the father. The drawback of this reading is that the rejecting son excelled no less than Freud. Different cause, same effect? That would be strange.

On strike

One surely senses a note of sacrilegious provocation in Joyce's reaction. What he has for Rome – that unmatched belle of history and Western art – is ostensibly only contempt . . . a *lèse-majesté*. Moreover, by identifying himself with the artist – with the definite article – he claims that his tastes carry as much weight as tradition. Without batting an eyelid, in the letter I just cited, he puts 'the impulses of (his) nature' (SL, p. 25) over and against the age-old precepts of the Church. Joyce the contester, then?

Likely he himself would not disagree, having written to Nora: 'My mind rejects the whole present social order and Christianity – home, the recognised virtues, classes of life, and religious doctrines' (ibid.). Except that he does not take issue only with the institutional apparatus of his time. With equal force, he denounces conventional sentiment and shared meanings. From the moment he arrives in Rome, he mocks prescribed emotions and describes with irony the young couple 'looking at it all round gravely from a sense of duty' (p. 91). All alone, Joyce takes it upon himself to make his cultural revolution, although in ways that short-circuit Marx – he seems never to have read beyond the first sentence of *Das Kapital*. His is no simple, banal, reformist protest that dreams of a new order. We see this in his supposed socialism which, for a while, he claims to adhere to, at the beginning of his stay in Rome. But for him it was never a concrete political option, and he willingly accepts to be called inconsistent since his socialism was in fact a temporary name for his 'intellectual strike' (p. 125), the expression he uses in his letter of 6 November 1906. To appeal to his supposed despondency is useless for understanding that his strike was aimed equally at the literature of his contemporaries. He mocks their hollow phrases, their conventional characters, their impoverished ways, the fact that 'they always keep beating about the bush' (p. 137), in short, their impotence in approaching the real through literature. He finally says that he has no wish to 'codify [himself] as anarchist or socialist or revolutionary' (p. 152), for they are all prescriptions from institutions he deems intolerable.

Joyce is no prodigal son. He is like a frail David – he spoke quite often about his fragility – facing the Goliath of the entire edifice of discourse on his own. For him the Father is just one puppet among others. Contemptuous of the mendacity of appearances – if one gives that name to the edifice of representations that, in each culture, are offered up by the Symbolic to the credulity and admiration of men – he puts in question all the products of civilisation that order and orient subjective reality.

But it is not only with a visceral hatred that the young 'artist' rejects the discourse of family, Church, University, Ireland, along with all the values the discourse carries which ring hollow to his ears. His *Nego* is an act, sustained and assumed, a rupture that goes beyond the simple feeling of resentment, because feelings . . . lie. Joyce's *Nego* does not lie. He turns the Latin tongue against itself, as Jacques Aubert says, and it is this reversal that turns resentment into an ethical act. How pertinent here is Lacan's remark that each one chooses the *lalangue* he speaks, even if he speaks the same idiom as others. Moreover, one creates it: 'One creates a tongue, inasmuch as, from one instant to the next, one endows it with meaning, one gives it a little nudge, without which it would not be a living tongue' (S, p. 114). To be sure, he exalts art in comparison to the common discourse that follows trends. But – in spite of a few nods to Ibsen and Yeats – the art is nevertheless an art to come: his own.

Put another way, for the one who had no wish 'to serve', there was an act, which cleared a space and cut away what were for him the two roots of his origin: the Church and Ireland. Without a doubt, he was rooted in them. He says so himself: 'It is a curious thing, do you know, Cranly said dispassionately, how your mind is supersaturated with the religion in which you say you disbelieve' (PAYM, p. 185). Yes, but he also said: 'I left the Catholic Church'. As for his ethnicity, he denounces it violently – the whole of *Portrait* is a torrent – but he does not disown it. 'This race and this country, this life produced me' (PAYM, p. 156).

And he evokes 'his ancestors' (ibid.) who reneged on their language and accepted the occupation, before promising – in 'an assertion of anticipated certainty' (É, p. 197) – 'to forge in the smithy of my soul the uncreated conscience of my race' (PAYM, p. 196). Belief in the uncreated conscience of his race is a great illusion, says Lacan. Indeed, but what is important here is the conjugation of the act of rupture, by which he separates himself from the race of his forebears, with the promise of restitution by the son.

This negation obviously imposes obligations that reach even as far as the treatment of *lalangue*. Consider the words he lends to Stephen Hero, his spokesman when it comes to his literary vocation. 'He was determined to fight with every energy of soul and body against any possible consignment to what he now regarded as the hell of hells – the region, otherwise expressed, wherein everything is found to be obvious [. . .]' (SH, p. 30). Here then is Joyce's *bête noire:* the enshrining of received beliefs and shared meanings: those of the Catholic Church, Home Rule for Ireland, together with the very essentials of English literature. In brief, the fat belly of the commonplace, for which eventually he will be the literary gravedigger. How could he love Rome, that quintessential city of dissembling? Instead, he offered his verdict for the new era: 'So let the ruins rot' (SL, p. 115).

The seriousness of Joyce's position should be judged less on what he said – any rebellious spirit can declaim – than on his know-how as an artist and the logic of his life. I will come back to this. In any case, his was not the inspired, stigmatising, reform-minded path of a Rousseau. It was, in contrast, a corrosive work that begins with a decisive *Nego*. In Rome, Joyce remembers that his mother called him a 'mocker' (SL, p. 132). Very likely and without any awareness, she had perceived the first signs of the irony he used to make himself master of the 'city of discourse', (Aé, p. 375) enough at least to get that most impregnable of institutions – the taste of the time – to bend to his wishes. The terms 'negativism', whose psychiatric usage is well-known, seems to me appropriate for descriptive purposes, but it has the disadvantage of suppressing the choice of the *Nego* which, for Joyce, was a position he worked out gradually, step by step, consciously: a constant work in progress that he accepted. I referred to his rejection of the commonplace, 'hell of hells', his search for an epiphanic beyond. But this puts him less on the side of mystical revelation than on the side of the search for the new, for the place from which the artist can originate a breakaway writing. More about this later. He describes – speaking of Stephen of course – a subject that is positioned outside of any influence, without any 'states of mind.' 'He was egoistically determined that nothing material [. . .] no bond of association or impulse or tradition should hinder him from working out the enigma of his position in his own way' (SH, p. 209).

There follow some remarks about his father – nefarious – and his mother – useless. This has nothing to do with a subject simply in revolt, for whom, despite protests and rebellion, the Other (friends, father, mother, tradition) is still supposed to know, or to be cause of the subject's enigmas. What we have in Joyce is an emancipated subject, separated from the injunctions of the Other, one who ferociously rejects the voice that commands and the norm that guides. There are numerous examples:

> While his mind had been pursuing its intangible phantoms and turning in irresolution from such pursuit he had heard about him the constant voices of his father and of his masters, urging him to be a gentleman above all things and urging him to be a good catholic above all things. These voices had now come to be hollow-sounding in his ears. When the gymnasium had been opened he had heard another voice urging him to be strong and manly and healthy and when the movement towards national revival had begun to be felt in the college yet another voice had bidden him to be true to his country and help to raise up her language and tradition. In the profane world, as he foresaw, a worldly voice would bid him raise up his father's fallen state by his labours and, meanwhile, the voice of his school comrades urged him to be a decent fellow . . .
>
> (*PAYM*, p. 63).

This sensitivity to the heteronomy of the voice of the Other, this fundamental rejection that reverses the submission of the weak, reaches to the level of a rejection assumed by the free man 'whose destiny was to be elusive of social and religious orders' (PAYM, p. 124). In the words of Stephen's companion: 'He is the only man I see [. . .] that has an individual mind' (PAYM, p. 155). Lacan endorses this viewpoint. The young man indeed identifies with the *individual*, positioning himself as the exception who says '*no*' to all the signifiers of the Other and even . . . to its language. On this point, we must read in *Portrait* the invaluable conversation with the rector around the words 'retain', 'pouring', and 'funnel', also briefly mentioned in *Stephen Hero*. It culminates in the radicalness of the following remarks: 'The language in which we are speaking is his before it is mine . . . his language, so familiar and so foreign, will always be for me an acquired speech. I have not made or accepted its words. My voice holds them at bay. My soul frets in the shadow of his language' (PAYM, p. 146).

It is true that, very briefly, suggestion seems to have worked for the young Stephen, for example, during the religious retreat following the sermon about Hell. The key to this particular moment, this moment of weakness, of opening to the divine Other, appears in the idea of the soul giving itself up to God. The 'surrender' that Joyce uses to evoke the wedding of the soul to its master, is more than a giving up, more than a handing over. In its connotations, at once military and sexual, it is not without evoking an ephemeral, mystical temptation.

But this was not his path – we have evidence for this; for him, mysticism was not even so much as a velleity. If he was an exception, it was not by way of consent but by way of sustained rejection, which is not to be confused with the adolescent's censorious revolt, traditionally considered to be a rite of passage. The adolescent's revolt may also challenge the reality of fathers and, more generally, everything that preceded them, but it does so in the name of the very ideals they transmitted and which belong precisely to the Other. Lacan writes this *I(A)*, the ideal of the Other. Nor is this a choice of method, the choice of a Descartes who, equally nourished in the best schools, suspended belief in the whole of received knowledge in order to find a path of certitude, that of his *cogito*. Engaged solely in a thought exercise, Descartes, as far as his conduct was concerned, relied on conformity to his 'provisional' morality; and as far as thought was concerned, on the guarantee of the supposed subject of knowledge, his God who is not a deceiver. Joyce's radicalism is nevertheless only one aspect of the choice he made. According to Lacan, his path was also characterised by 'sound logic' (S, p. 4).

A sound logic

This way of approaching truth, so incredulous, so ironic, which seeks to retain from truth only what is most singular, is nevertheless not all there is to Joyce's heretical choice. He is not content to reduce truth by way of irony or the letter of his writing. According to Lacan, he takes it on also by way of logic. This is why he can be called '*Joyce the Symptom*'. This aspect of Lacan reading Joyce – formulated in *The Sinthome* (18 November 1975), and taken up again in *Joyce le symptôme II* – requires explanation, in contrast to what I have called Joyce's negativism, which is displayed explicitly. Where, then, do we find this characteristic – 'sound logic' – since Joyce in no way claims to be a logician?

We can note that Lacan credits himself with heresy by way of sound logic, and not without reason. For he, too, can serve as an example: in the field of speech and language where psychoanalysis operates, the real is reached by logic. For many years, he utilised the logic inherent in language and the logician's approach to undermine false beliefs and reach – by way of the matheme and proof – what in language is the most real of truth, namely the half-saying, to which truth is condemned by the structure of language, at the very heart of the lie about its impotence to reach the Real outside the Symbolic. He, too, was led in the end to a sort of analytic pseudo *cogito:* I think, I think but not without the signifiers that represent me, I think, therefore 'there is Oneness' [*y a d'l'Un*], not the two of the sexual relationship, and this 'I think' . . . is enjoyed.

In Joyce, it is easy to see that – with his exile – what is a serious choice reaches the level of act. Let us not forget that *Portrait* is the story of an extraction, culminating in a departure that inscribes the subject's position in the real and in the logic of his life. This is not the transitory exile of a well-to-do son with a return ticket in his pocket. Rather it is definitive, that of a son 'dispossessed' as much symbolically as materially. How, then, not to connect the character to the author. How, then, not to emphasise that Joyce himself, beyond all fear, with nothing but the certitude of his destiny – with his exile – put his signature on the seriousness of his choice. I could almost speak of 'exile without motive', (echoing a better-known expression) to stress that his motives were not situational. Neither Dublin nor his family nor his friends had rejected this young man. Nor did his art, or even Art with a capital 'A', demand another soil. It was not need, as in the case of so many of his compatriots; and it was not the call of the wider world that made him say 'I am leaving'. It was something else: the work of the rejection of *semblants*. Thus, Joyce made himself 'uprooted', forever beyond borders.

His signature radicalness of choice: this is what gives coherence to his position. But it is not enough to make for *sound logic*. Something else has to be added: the factor of time which, in 1945, Lacan called 'logical time' (É, pp. 161–76). Lacan implicitly refers to this when he says the function of haste can be seen in Joyce. For the subject called upon to make a decision, the 'certitude' of the act anticipates the 'moment of concluding', prepared for by the 'time for understanding'. In Joyce's case, it is 'anticipated certainty' that precipitates him into act, decisions that appear 'mad' in relation to reality, in the name of his destiny as a future artist. Here I refer not only to his exile. He himself is aware of it. As we saw above, when he resigns his post in Rome, he says: 'There is some element of sanity in this last mad performance of mine, I am sure' (SL, p. 150). But even haste is not enough, since 'sound logic' is judged by the conclusive move the haste anticipated. From his early years, Joyce hastened to position himself as *the artist*, with the definite article, the one and only. As for his haste, he probably does not perceive 'the logic it determines' (*J/L*, p. 34). But, Lacan tells us, this does not stop him 'portraying it as having more merit because it comes solely from his art' (ibid.) In other words, logic need not be explicit so long as it yields a conclusion. It is with *Ulysses* that this conclusion is established, by way of the know-how that finally provides the certitude of his *sinthome being*. This is Lacan's thesis. It was not enough to have produced all the texts that came before. Joyce needed to produce an '*eaube jeddard*, like *Ulysses*, that is a *jet d'art* on the *l'eaube scène* of logic itself' (ibid.). Once more – provided we do not allow ourselves to be intimated by the play with equivocations – we understand that Lacan attributes to *Ulysses* a function that is more than simply literary, a logical function, which establishes Joyce, not only as the artist he claimed to be, but as 'the necessary son who does not stop conceiving himself writing himself' (ibid.). That is to say, the artist without a father, as such, uncreated. As Joyce himself says: 'the uncreated conscience of my race' (PAYM, p. 196). With *Ulysses*, James Joyce rises to the status of exception. Now, as any reader of Lacan knows, for the Freudian Oedipus that he rejected, Lacan substituted the function of exception as the logical condition for any functioning of discourse. Joyce's art will thus have brought him into the path of sound logic, the very logic that permitted him to sustain himself and, indeed, to win recognition as master in the city of discourse.

All in all, Joyce's heresy will have consisted in arriving at truth via a double pathway: the *Nego* conjugated with sound logic; and time, a course of time, not for understanding, but for producing *Ulysses*. This course of time will finally allow him to contain the *Nego*. This is what we shall see. And we will have understood that if the artist as exception makes up for the failure of the father, it also marks its unconditional character by establishing it as a place and putting Joyce's *sinthome-saying* there. If Joyce felt a calling to any mission, it was not to be a saviour. He saves only himself and does so without recourse to the '*hystoriette*' of Hamlet, who was much more talkative and totally lacking in heresy. It was thus without 'hystory', not even Homer's 'Ulysses', that James Joyce could create – against-Oedipus, if I may put it like that – his founding heresy.

Notes

1 This chapter is based on the lecture delivered as part of the Reading Texts Seminar, which I taught in the Collège clinique du Champ lacanien in Paris, 2011–2012.
2 The phrase is included in the 2016 English translation of the Seminar by Adrian Price.
3 I have kept the spelling of the transcriptions from the first lesson of the seminar, *sinthome*, which Lacan has just introduced, rather than *symptom*. However, I note that the 'agency of the letter' produced by Lacan as the play of metaphor and metonymy, can indeed disseminate the jouissance of the symptom in the signifier, displace the signifier and thus even multiply it, but it is not of the order of the *saying-sinthome*.

Chapter 4

An Original Diagnosis

'Joyce the symptom, to be heard like *Jésus la caille:* that is his name', (J/L, p. 31) a name that differentiates him from *Jésus la caille* and, to be sure, from everyone else. *Jésus la caille* is the eponymous main character of a novel written in 1914 by Francis Carco. At the close of the nineteenth century in Paris, the 'jesuses' were male prostitutes, who gave each other feminine names. The character, *Jésus la caille*, is thus named for his jouissance symptom. It is a proper name – the true one – applicable to one and only one, with no namesakes, and therefore different from the simple patronym. It can only be the name of a singularity, whether of desire or of jouissance: in other words, the name of a symptom. Thus we talk about 'The Ratman' or 'The Wolfman' for Freud's cases; but also 'The Cursed One', or 'Zorro the Avenger'. With Joyce, we have something different. The symptom: this is his name. But it does not tell us the name of his singular jouissance, nor about the symptom he has. For example, Lacan does not call him '*Joyce l'élangues*', an expression from Philippe Sollers that Lacan cites at the beginning of his seminar, even though we have no doubt that he uses *lalangue* with a totally singular jouissance, quite close to what we would think of as manic elation. Rather, Joyce *is* symptom, even *sinthome*, according to Lacan, indeed a symptomatology, as well as being heretical. This is a diagnosis of structure, distinctly not neurosis. But is it then psychosis? The issue is more complex than often recognised, whether one replies in the affirmative, as Lacanians often do, or *a priori* in the negative, following the suggestion of Michel Foucault, for whom a single work would suffice to rule this out. Certainly, Lacan asked the question: '. . . yes or no, was Joyce mad . . .' (S, p. 62). But if we reread *The Sinthome*, the seminar he devotes to Joyce, we can see how careful he is not to take a decision on this epithet by way of a 'yes' or a 'no', especially given that 'epithets push towards yea or nay' (S, p. 101).

Sinthome, not delusion

What he proposes, as he himself formulates it, is to consider that 'Joyce's case corresponds to a way of making up for the knot's coming undone' (S, p. 71). Now, in the schema of the Borromean knot that Lacan was using at the time, and into which the old clinical categories had been translated, neurosis and psychosis are approached in terms of knotting and unknotting. In other words, when Lacan talks about *suppléance*, he is excluding the binary response of 'yes' or 'no' and introducing the idea of a knotting other than that assured by the *Père-sinthome* (*Paternal-sinthome*). Certainly he assumed that the major condition for psychosis was there, namely deficiency in what he called the *sinthome-Père* (*Father-as-sinthome*). But a supplementation has been produced, forged by the know-how of the artist. This is why I stated some time ago that Joyce acutely illustrates Lacan's formulation when, at the end of *The Sinthome*, he states that one can 'just as well bypass [the father], on the condition that one make use of it' (S, p. 116).

Note that Lacan does not use the term 'psychosis' in this seminar. He only asks whether or not Joyce was mad. But the madman and the psychotic are not the same. In 1946, in his '*Presentation on Psychical Causality*' (É, pp. 123–60), where he puts the unconscious imago in the position of cause, and where he approaches madness by way of the imaginary phenomenon of belief, Lacan defines the madman as the one who 'thinks he really is something', just like the dandy born into a rich family. He adds that 'a man who thinks he is king is mad, a king who thinks he is a king is no less so' (S, p. 139). Indeed, we – like the madman – believe, but what we believe in is . . . the Other. 'Believing in' the Other is no less delusional than believing in oneself. Both are cases of dominance over the Real of Imaginary-Symbolic fabrications. But, insofar as the Other of language is inherent in our reality, we can misrecognise it. In the end, Lacan says: 'everyone is delusional' (Lacan, 1979, p. 278), and he who once said, 'one cannot choose to go mad', meaning psychotic, clarifies, with his question about Joyce, that going mad is not a privilege. Here 'mad' means delusional; and if everyone is delusional, one understands that this is not a diagnosis. It has to do with the Imaginary. On the occasion of Jacques Aubert's lecture, he makes the question even more precise: did Joyce believe himself to be a saviour? This is not very easy to answer, since we have only Joyce's writings, not his speech. For, 'when one writes, one may indeed touch on the Real, but not the true' (S, p. 64). What of Joyce's speech do we have? Nothing direct. A lot of testimony about his person has been gathered, of which Ellmann made great use. But as for Joyce talking about himself, there is only written speech, well thought out, from *Stephen Hero* to *Portrait*, with an interval of about ten years between them. And then there are the letters.

Why this question of a possible *Joyce the delusional*, at the very moment when Lacan has already advanced his thesis of *Joyce the symptom*, which is a different thing? Is it because the saviour delusion – which more than anything else throws open the question of the father – seems to respond to the foreclosure with an attempt to save the Father, albeit Imaginarily, whereas the *sinthome* pertains to the Real? Assuredly yes. For, regarding the deficiency of the Father, Lacan has no doubts or questions, he asserts it, without nuance. It is surely a point worth looking into, given the clinical relevance of what we know about Joyce's father. I will come back to this. But what Lacan was seeking to clarify over the course of the seminar and what he was exploring here concerned what Joyce made of it, how he responded to it.

Now Freud had already situated delusion as an attempt at healing, a solution to the illness of psychosis, which he considered to be libidinal, marked by withdrawal of investment in objects. 'I do not love him' (Lacan, 1990a, p. 10). This is how Lacan translates Freud's way of conjugating what underlies the various forms of delusion, the function of which is precisely to restore libidinal connection, notably in the form of persecution or erotomania. Commenting on Freud's Schreber case in '*On a Question Prior to Any Possible Treatment of Psychosis*' (É, pp. 445–88), Lacan does not disagree, situating Schreber's delusion as an elaboration that permits him to move from the position of one persecuted by God to the position of wife of God, thanks to which the Imaginary relation to the Other and to reality could be stabilised and become tolerable again. Thus, from the beginning, the delusion has been viewed as a salubrious response to the defect of foreclosure. But we are well aware that there is more than one step between the attempt at cure via lucubration and the path toward *suppléance* through the logic of the symptom.

Furthermore, Lacan's commentary on the Schreber case is entirely constructed on a presupposition excluded by the Borromean knot: the presupposition of the Imaginary's subordination to the Symbolic and the 'induction' effects of the signifier on the Imaginary. 'Induction': this is Lacan's term. Such effects allowed him, for example, to say that without the Other, the subject cannot sustain himself even in the narcissistic position; to situate the signifier of the phallus as the effect of the paternal metaphor; and to conclude for Schreber that 'this symbolic determination is demonstrated in the form in which the Imaginary structure comes to be restored' (É, p. 474). But contrary to this, with the Borromean knot, Lacan does not stop repeating – doubtless because too many times in the past he had said the opposite – that the three consistencies are autonomous and equivalent, that is to say, there is no subordination; and only by way of their knotting, in the relation of each to the others, can they have an effect. We need to follow step by step how Lacan's best-known theses were, and needed to be, modified. He made sure to alter the one about delusion by telling us that 'everyone is delusional' and therefore it is not a privilege. Indeed, everyone, mad or not, is armed with a little private story, of his own making or borrowed, depending upon the case, which assures him of his being by inscribing him under a signifier and giving him a shape. But in all cases, this linguistic lucubration tells lies about the Real. If we notice when Lacan posed the question ('was Joyce mad?') – it was on 10 February 1976, at a time when the thesis of Joyce the symptom had already been formulated – we can conclude that Lacan was not questioning the fact of Joyce's *suppléance*. Rather it was about his Imaginary, perhaps even about the effects of his *suppléance sinthome* on his Imaginary, this Imaginary (to which Lacan returns in the last lesson), that was a bit too free from the knot's netting. This does not mean that he lacked the Imaginary. A question, therefore, about the nature of the *suppléance*, and the range of its consequences, to which I will return.

Let us recall here that, in his 1967 text *'La méprise du sujet supposé savoir'* (Aé, pp. 329–40), Lacan grouped together James Joyce, Moses, and Meister Eckhart, a trio of fathers, not of the Church, but of what he called 'deo-logue', to distinguish it from gods one believes in, such as the god of the philosophers, the supposed subject of knowledge latent in any theory from Descartes to the theologians; or from the god of the prophets, the god of speech and will who speaks through them. Thus for Lacan, contrary to Freud, God is not an illusion produced by human frailty. God exists, whether or not we believe in him, necessitated by the structure of language. He depends, not on faith, but on the logic of language and discourse. Hence Lacan's successive formulations, depending on whether he is referring to language or to discourse: 'God is unconscious', a hole in language, the *Urverdrängung*, the personified chasm of primordial repression or, as Lacan puts it, the chasm 'made person'. But he is also *the saying* that exists from language, the *dieure-Père*, since '*the said* (in its linguistic form) does not happen without *the saying*' (L'é, p. 8). We can understand why Moses is placed within this logic of the *dieure-le-père* since, in addition to the Tablets of the Law, he transmitted the famous formula whose translation remains so controversial: 'I am that I am'. A hole if ever there was one, according to Lacan. No doubt he put Meister Eckhart there on account of his negative theology, which makes of God the Unpredictable One par excellence. Once again, a hole. As for Joyce, in 1967, it seems Lacan had put the reason for his inclusion on hold, making it explicit and specific only in texts from 1975. But Lacan was already indicating that going from Freud's 'deo-logue' – which marks out a place for God-the-Father (Lacan's 'Name-of-the-Father') – to talking about *Dieure-père* changes everything. Already, with respect to Joyce, we are very far from a simple diagnosis of psychosis. In 1975, Lacan substitutes symptomatology for '*diologie*'. We can understand this based on the fact that, in the meantime, he had formulated the father as a symptomatic solution. The confirmation is in Joyce who did not so much believe himself to be, as make himself, 'artificer' (S, p. 56). This being so, it matters little what he might have thought of himself. The artificer will have, as it were, stood in for what one imagines to be the supreme artist, God himself. Here is the distance from believing to doing, from Imaginary to Real.

Joyce is a very special case of the *self-made man*. In general, those who speak are anchored in their childhoods. At the structural level, the presence of the child in the adult comes from the fact that what has been inscribed in a contingent manner becomes necessity, never ceasing to write itself. This is what occurs in the repetition of trauma, and also in the symptom-*fixion*'s indelibility in the Real of jouissance. It is the fault of no one, coming rather from the impossible that language creates, what Lacan called *troumatisme*. Consider the saying of nomination, the saying which *knots-names man*, if I may pastiche Lacan who pastiched Joyce. When we receive an analysand, generally the knot is already there, 'already made', as Lacan put it. It dates from infancy and extends into the adult. Whence the idea that, at best, through the signifying production of analysis, we will be able to correct the knot with various sutures and splices. This shows us that the analyst is neither a father nor a substitute for a father, nor a *dieure*. His apophantic, oracular saying does not produce the *sinthome*. It was already there, contrary to what one sometimes hears.

In Joyce, on the other hand, there is clearly no original knot, a 'failing', says Lacan. But failing can be corrected. The *naming sinthome* is something unconditioned. But if the condition is absent, it can be supplemented and, in Joyce's case, it is. According to Lacan, as I have said before, this occurs by way of Joyce's making himself a 'necessary son' (J/L, p. 34), a son with no genealogy. One sees the paradox. Something without genealogy is named by a genealogical term – son – a son as uncreated as 'the spirit of his race', according to Joyce. This is a true invention which seems to have required time, crystallising during his adolescence, the development of which we can read about in *A Portrait of the Artist*. We cannot ignore how important it was to Joyce to narrate this, with *Ulysses* confirming his anticipated certainty. So it was that Joyce did without the father, renaming himself by means of a *Father-saying*, a *dieure*, with the whole question coming down to knowing to what extent the substitute saying works as well as the saying of the father.

What failing?

As I have already indicated, Lacan does not say that Joyce is psychotic. But he does assert rather categorically what he himself had posited as the major condition for psychosis: the failing of the father. It took little more than this for some to stumble into rashly saying that this was a case of psychosis. But let us take a closer look. What reasons do we have for considering Joyce's father to have been a failure? But before we get to that, just what is paternal failure? The term is there but we cannot take it as self-evident, given that the person who proposed it is the very same who, after reformulating the Freudian Oedipus with the Paternal Metaphor, moved to an insistent, repeated, often virulent criticism of this same Oedipus and, beyond that, claimed that he could establish the analytic discourse without recourse to the Name-of-the-Father.[1] Failing, then. But what kind and how do we know it?

Can we understand this at the level of family history? One would think so, for Lacan does not hesitate to call upon biography; and he describes John Joyce, father of James, in quite vigorous terms: 'A boozing father, who was more or less a Fenian' (S, p. 7). This refers to the name of an Irish insurrectionist movement which Joyce wrote about in an article entitled: 'Fenianism: The Last Fenian' (1907). Of Joyce's father, Jacques Aubert has said: he was less Fenian than feigner. The homophony of the verb 'to feign' clearly introduces doubt about the seriousness of John Joyce's support for Parnell. It also evokes another homophony, between Fenian and *fainéant* (lazy), which John Joyce surely was. Lacan goes on: 'His father distinguishes himself precisely as – ummm – as what we might call an unworthy father, a failing father . . .' (S, p. 55). And further: 'Let's say his father was never a father to him? Not only did he teach him nothing, he neglected pretty much everything, save for relying on the good Jesuit fathers, the Church diplomatic' (S, p. 72). He even speaks of a 'paternal abdication' (ibid.).

Shocking remarks when compared to those of the very same Lacan over a period of twenty years, from 'On a Question Prior' to *Seminar XXII: R.S.I.*, concerning the relation between fathers and foreclosure in their sons. Nevertheless, it is one and the same person who, in the postscript to 'On a Question Prior', denounces the father who is too much of an educator and much enjoys mocking those who think they can diagnose foreclosure by some failing of the person of the father. Indeed, he speaks ironically of 'paternal failing' – about which 'there has been no shortage of accounts of every kind' (É, p. 481), '. . . the range of which is unsettling, including as it does the thundering father, the easy-going father, the all-powerful father, the humiliated father, the rigid father, the pathetic father, the stay-at-home father, and the father on the loose . . .' (p. 482). In short, he stigmatises the portraits of those supposedly unworthy fathers by returning them to the register of the Imaginary conceived as non-causal, whereas the agency of the Name-of-the-Father, purely symbolic, is causal. What a contrast to what we can read in *The Sinthome*, to which I have just referred. If this is not a contradiction, then there is something like a reversal that requires elucidation.

With the paternal metaphor, one could already say of the Name-of-the-Father what he later says of God: he is unconscious. In any case, this is not a directly observable phenomenon. It was supposed to be conditioned by the *Bejahung* Freud spoke about, a kind of primordial assent that institutes the signifier, whose presence or lack is manifest only in the consequences. From then on, foreclosure had to account for the structure of linguistic phenomena and their correlates in the field of the Real, about which Lacan was already saying '. . . it is the domain of that which subsists outside of symbolisation' (É, p. 324). Foreclosure was inferred from that. In other words, failure cannot be diagnosed on the basis of adherence to the norms of the conjugal family or on the personal characteristics of fathers (or mothers). It is not a failure of the father, but the lack 'of the signifier itself' (É, p. 465). *Voilà!* This is what justifies the moment of irony. Yet while he was criticising descriptions of failing fathers, Lacan was not excluding – however subtly – the possible 'devastating effects of the paternal figure' (É, p. 482), even portraying this in the father of Schreber. Nothing of the Imaginary determines these ravaging effects, only the relation of a father to the Law, which Lacan writes with a capital letter, to distinguish it from the everyday meaning of 'laws'. Hence the risk that he evokes for a father – the one who makes himself a legislator, or paragon of some ideal, or master in education or politics – to find himself in a position deserving of censure or fraud in relation to the signifier of the Law. The argument was solid. But it does not at all apply to the figure of Joyce's father, who did not give a fig for pedants. Besides, what Lacan says about him in *The Sinthome* does not belong to this register. 'Boozer', 'Fenian', 'he taught his son nothing': all expressions that evoke failures to meet bourgeois norms, as if one would expect sobriety, a taste for work, even the virtue of transmitting an education from a father worthy of this name. So strange for Lacan.

However this may be, if we turn for a moment to descriptive history, the trajectory of John Joyce's life is one of inexorable decline – financial, social, and personal – in which his family was dragged down along with him. If we follow Richard Ellmann, there is every reason to consider John Joyce as irresponsible, leading his family into poverty and ruin. In the space of thirteen years (1881–1893), ten children and three miscarriages; the oldest, who came before James, did not survive. Not at all unusual for the time. But what was unusual: at the birth of each child, a property was sold, such that in the end nothing was left (Ellmann, 1982, p. 37). Flashy and emotional, a *bon vivant* fond of drink and boisterous conviviality, concerned with what others thought of him, immeasurably vain and egotistical, tyrannical but inconsistent, according to his son James. He also imposed on his family his social passions, his political militancy, his taste and talent for music, song, and theatre. How can we not recall the description in *Stephen Hero* of his most intimate passions, including, from the beginning, a hatred for his wife and her family, so present that, daily and dangerously, it invaded the household's evenings. How can we not recognise in this portrait of the artist's father the inverse of classical, bourgeois values? But neither Lacan nor psychoanalysis invites us to make of 'work, family, fatherland' the paternal virtues par excellence. What, then, was his failing? Already we can say that it was not lack of love or appreciation for James, his second son, undoubtedly his favourite, who consoled him for the loss of the first. From early on, he had the highest opinion of James and wanted to give him the best possible education by entrusting him to the Jesuits, undoubtedly the best thing John James ever did. Stanislaus Joyce, in *My Brother's Keeper*, attests to this. James, out of everyone in the family, was always the most attached and most conciliatory towards his father. According to Stanislaus, who consciously hated his father, this was because James, off to the Jesuits at the age six, in his most formative years knew only the family's fortunate time, the time of good relations, affluence, renown, theatre and music. Had not James, barely six years old, participated with his parents in a song recital? What then was lacking?

When we turn to Lacan's elaborations subsequent to the paternal metaphor, we see that everything changed in his teaching in terms of the weight of the Name and of fathers, from the moment when the Names of the Father appeared in the plural. Indeed, if there are Names, how can we avoid defining the function, in the singular, independently of them; and, correlatively, posing the question of knowing under what condition a father, any father, can or cannot be a support for that function. I note in addition that, at the end of the seminar on *Anxiety*, in the last lessons before the summer of 1963 – that is, just before planning for the never-completed seminar *Les non-dupes errent* – Lacan, for the first time, if I am not mistaken, after virulently criticising the Freudian Oedipus, considers the function of desire in *a* father. He takes up the same theme ten years later in *R.S.I.* (21 January 1975), where he defines a father that is a 'model of the function'.

So why not compare the figure of Joyce's father to the 'model of the function' father described by Lacan in this lesson? He states that for a father to be a model, that is, a support for the function – in other words, that there not be an effect of foreclosure – two conditions are required: a symptom condition of jouissance and a condition of saying. The first condition is required for everyone, on account of the absence of any sexual relation that could be enunciated in speech or inscribed in the language of the unconscious. As I have already indicated, it is the symptom that makes up for this absence, this 'ab-sex'. From this it follows that, for a father to be model of the function, he must have the symptom of *père-version*, the father version of the symptom which, in order to make up for the nonrelation, establishes a specific link to a woman.

'It matters little if he has symptoms, provided he adds to them the paternal *père-version*, a woman as cause of his desire whom he acquires for the purpose of giving him children . . .'. (R.S.I., 21 January 1975). This formulation seems to suggest something like a desire for a child, a desire for paternity. Lacan adds: 'whether he wants to or not, he takes paternal care' (ibid.) of the children. Thus, it is not about what pleases him. A new notion for Lacan, this 'paternal care'. We have to assume it is different from the better known maternal care and, moreover, that Lacan is not confounding it with what I refer to as the bourgeois virtues of a *paterfamilias*. Bringing together some diverse developments in Lacan, my hypothesis is that paternal care can only be the nomination that is constitutive of lineage, given that in this same period Lacan was also saying that the father is the father of the name (Soler, 2001).

The second condition Lacan mentions is more difficult to elucidate and could lend itself to misunderstanding. It concerns the father's speech, which must remain in the realm of *mi-dire (half-saying)*. For the children, this *half-saying* operates 'exceptionally and in the best of cases to maintain under repression, under happy half-saying, the version of *père-version* that belongs to him' (R.S.I., 21 January 1975). With the word 'repression', what is evoked is the veil thrown over the symptomatic jouissance of the father. This is a theme Lacan often approached, most notably when he emphasised the weight of the father's sins on his descendants. Are there sins other than jouissance? The father's true failing, according to this thesis, would be in his potential for obscenity, for a jouissance too present on the surface in his speech. Nevertheless, Lacan insists: 'Normality is not the paternal virtue par excellence, but only the just right half-god . . . the just right not-said' (ibid.). To conclude: a father owes it to himself not to be a *dieure* (a saying-god). He has but one duty: to be a *mi-dieure* (a god of half-saying).

Curiously, Lacan takes up again something he said before about the Schreber case, which I mentioned above, and which seems to have nothing to do with half-saying: 'Nothing worse than the father who proffers his law on everything. Above all, no educator father, but instead one who steps back from any magisterium' (ibid.). Neither an agent of social order, nor a collaborator with those who police and maintain it. But why? What is the connection to half-saying? Is it what Michel Foucault perceived so well, that the one who designates, even hunts down, prohibited jouissances thus makes them transgressive and thereby opens their path? Lacan, following Luther, often repeated: one needs the Law to be a sinner. The ambiguity of 'spoken commandments', the ambiguity of prohibitions, wherein sins are detailed and temptations stirred up, by this very naming, indicate the pathways of sin. If this is how it works, is it not easy to see the link to the duty of half-saying? The supercilious educator-father, by designating sins, would sin against the duty of half-saying that Lacan linked to his function.

In any case, what we see here is that a father – worthy of the name, support of a function – is defined without reference to social norms. It is true that the first condition, electing a woman for the purpose of giving him children, does closely resemble what is promoted as the conjugal, heterosexual family, a bit worse for wear today when families need not be heterosexual. Nevertheless, this objection does not hold, since Lacan does not make this the norm for the Father-symptom. He only seeks to grasp how those who have this symptom affect their descendants.

By the yardstick of half-saying, how does the father of James Joyce measure up? Discretion regarding his jouissances was surely not his forte, if we are to believe Stanislaus, not to speak of James himself, both of whom described him as a *jouisseur*, whose ego overflowed with satisfied obscenity, whose tastes and passions were daily and proudly displayed to family and society, even as he was inconsistent about everything and responsible for nothing. Yet this obscenity is not relevant to his *père-version*. The question is rather to know whether or not this included a woman acquired to give him children . . . all appearances point to this but not more, for this is a matter not of reality, but of desire. According to Ellmann, the reality was that John Joyce's family married him off to temper his youthful misbehaviours. We can only assume that his hatred for his wife and her family, so loud, so vigilant, quasi-paranoid, never resting, far from half-said, in no way disposed toward the naming of a half-said paternal desire. Failing, then.

But for all that, we have not advanced. Certainly, we can picture a deficient, failing father. But any deduction as to the effects on a child of a father who lacks the father-symptom would be more than risky. The relation of transmission, whether or not it is paternal, is never a simple relation of cause to effect. All the more as the Father is substitutable, both as a signifier and as a carrier of nomination. To stay in the realm of biography, the good Jesuit fathers came perfectly recommended, if only Joyce would have been able to consent. Proposing the priesthood to him, they themselves, if only for a moment, seem to have believed he could.

'De facto foreclosure'

Happily, with respect to this confusion about paternal transmission, Lacan, I believe, put forward something else, but doubtless too discreetly. He spoke about a '*de facto Verwerfung*' (S, p. 62). *De facto foreclosure.* This expression is surprising. What does it mean? Not too long ago, I commented on it in my seminar at Sainte-Anne Hospital, under the welcoming auspices of Dr Françoise Gorog. From that time on, I have raised the problem, even encouraged one of the participants to present a paper on the theme. But for me the question remains unresolved. To begin with, there are two ways of understanding this expression. On the one hand, we can take 'fact' in the ordinary sense of something observed. But then we are far from the structure of experience, and the expression sends us back to descriptive biography, the inadequacy of which I just noted. For any facts of the father's biography, it would be necessary to specify how they affected the being of the child; and even if these effects are attested to in the child's biography, how can it be ascertained that these effects are the result of the father? On the other hand, we can take this expression as a simple redundancy in relation to the very definition of foreclosure: the absence of a signifier, but this is always the case, that there is or there is not. Thus, 'de facto foreclosure' would bring nothing new.

As I now understand it, this expression cannot be separated from other statements Lacan made in parallel to it, on the same pages of the seminar, about the term 'fact'. He reiterates: there is no fact except by being said. Quite rigorously, this applies to 'de facto foreclosure'. The fact of foreclosure is assured only by being said. And by whom, if not by the one whose structure we question. But it was still necessary to add that whatever 'is uttered here de facto [. . .] remains suspended from the enigma of the enunciation' (S, p. 10). Had not Lacan already said: 'That one says remains forgotten in what is said . . .' (L'é, p. 5). A phrase that is murderous for any inclination to ontology. To anyone who says 'being is', we can always reply 'you said it' (p. 49), the minimum formula for analytic interpretation, because what we aim at is the 'that one says'. For what is to be read in speech is not 'what it says' but 'that it says' (Aé, p. 450). Put another way, it is from Joyce's text – from the son's saying – that we can diagnose *de facto foreclosure*. A father's 'abdication', insofar as it is causal, regardless of the father's other traits, is nothing but what is said of this 'abdication' and only happens with the son's enunciation. And this is logical when one bears in mind that no signifier, even a name, is sustained without 'assent'. Joyce himself uses this term, which gives great weight to a notion, often difficult to handle but unavoidable in the clinic: the notion of the 'unfathomable decision of being' (É, p. 145), which Lacan located at the origin of the clinical structures. It is occasionally evoked, but without a gauge for its true scope, without success in using it. One is then forced to give up; and this occurs, without doubt, because there has been insufficient detachment from Lacan's first formulations, which made of the Name-of-the-Father a signifier in the Other, a sort of Other of the Other, that gives the Law of the Other, or else failure ensues.[2] Thus, in large part, the Lacanian theory of psychosis came to be oriented by the idea that, not only does its cause come from the Other, but from the Other as supported by 'small others', namely the parental figures. Have we forgotten that the Other, written with a capital letter, is not a person but a place, the Other scene, as Freud called it, just as 'extimate' to the subject as are those small others? Certainly, the subject is formed in the place of the Other, but the heteronomy of language does not relieve him of responsibility, that is to say, of his response. Too often foreclosure is thought of as suffered, something simply passed down to the subject across generations. David Graham Cooper even asserted that it took two generations to produce psychosis in the third. But *de facto foreclosure*, if the fact is suspended from the said, which does not exist without the saying, this is an enunciative, enacted foreclosure. A foreclosure that is not to be inferred from its effects, as I was saying about the Name of the Father, because it is, so to speak resolute, just as one speaks about resolute desire. To put it rather bluntly, it is not because of the father, but because of the son. Here one must be very precise in distinguishing which biographical conditions are more or less favourable to the concept of causality properly so called. In this area, Joyce gives an exceptional clinical presence to the unfathomable subjective choice. I will allow myself to put it this way: 'the subject supposed' (as we read in *l'Etourdit*, I will come back to this) to the saying.

What, then, in Joyce's text marks this enunciative foreclosure? Several features. He bore witness to some of them in the attempt he made to 'decipher his own riddle'. Others are discernible in his savoir-faire as an artist.

According to Lacan, in the figure of Stephen Dedalus, he testifies to receiving a 'calling' (S, p. 73). The word has religious resonances, but it is appropriate, and one feels this in *A Portrait of the Artist*. Called to compensate for . . . his own stated rejection of the father, well beyond the person of *his* father. 'Tasked' with the father, Joyce gives himself the mission of 'support[ing] this father for him to subsist' (S, p. 13). It is tempting to connect these affirmations to the father he knew in an irrevocably fallen state, whose long descent into poverty is doubtless not unrelated to the theme of the fall that runs from the beginning to the end of *Finnegans Wake*. And *Portrait*, too, ends with an invocation of the Name: 'Old father, old artificer, stand me now and ever in good stead' (PAYM, p. 196). But, as Lacan says, the *artificer*, the artisan of savoir-faire, is Joyce himself. I would add that this is not a case of 'get out so that I can get in'. The place was certainly free, but not without his having been there already, doing the hollowing himself; not without excavating the site with his saying. It is worth noting that the theme of the father is omnipresent and quite clear in his works, particularly in *Ulysses*. He looks for a father, says Lacan, 'in the guise of he who is not to be found at any level whatsoever' (S, p. 55). He is not there. Nonetheless, there is a father – Bloom – made of the same material as himself, looking for a son. But to this father, Stephen lodges a protest 'that it is *really not for him*' (S, p. 55). John Joyce also looked for a son, one that would make his own deficiencies matter less. '*Ulysses* is the testimony to how Joyce remains deeply rooted in his father while still disowning him' (ibid.). A renegade vis-à-vis the father. This is not just any position. I have mentioned his decisive rejection of the discourse of the Other, his no less decisive aspiration toward a less stupid language, a less stupid saying, which would be his own. Here, the subjective, 'de facto' option is quite obvious, no doubt consistent with his primordial rejection of the father. In Joyce, this refusal of assent – which made him, willingly and decisively, into someone who is not to be duped – is all along perfectly perceptible. But in his art, in the space he cleared, he produces the *sinthome* as *suppléance*, that is, himself. Lacan names him the 'necessary son' who illustrates, beyond his family, 'what somewhere he calls *my country*, or better still, *the uncreated conscience of my race*' (S, p. 14). A strange, creationist takeover of John Joyce's Irish patriotism, which itself was too ineffectual to be anything but derisory. Thus, without knowing it, but through sound logic, Joyce will have demonstrated the necessity of the function of exception that is required for any discourse to stay in place. Thus, there is a solidarity between the act of saying, that I am going to call *Nego* of the father, and the act that his art carried and by which he makes himself *sinthome*. From *de facto foreclosure* to *suppléance*, which is also *de facto* in the sense I have described, there is the same subjective choice, as we shall see. Lacan called him 'the individual' (S, p. 147), as I said before. I will now turn to the various singularities that Lacan recognises in him.

Notes

1 Responding to Question No. 4 in *Radiophonie*.
2 See Lacan's postscript to *On a Question Prior* . . .

Chapter 5

Symptoms

What I want to stress here is the conjunction between '*de facto foreclosure*' and a *sinthome* that is not the father-version of the *sinthome*. The two together make *the individual*, and their conjunction is what sets Joyce apart from psychosis and also, it should be noted, from neurosis. How could this singular 'subjective constitution' (Aé, p. 373) not have repercussions for his other symptoms, his relationship to his body, to his partner, and to his children, all of which involve a configuration of desire and jouissance? Lacan singled out two of them: Joyce's specific relation to his wife, Nora, to whom he was linked without the father version of generalised perversion; and above all, the relation to his own body, from which, at the end of the seminar, Lacan diagnoses a 'slip of the knot' [*lapsus du noeud*] (S, p. 75), through an unknotting of the Imaginary.

Without the body

At the end of the seminar, Lacan advances his thesis of a 'slip of the knot', which would leave the Joycean Imaginary unknotted from the Symbolic and the Real and in some way free. This is the knot we can see in the lesson of 11 May 1976, where the Imaginary 'is not knotted in a Borromean way to what makes a chain of the real and the unconscious' (S, p. 131). Hence an Imaginary that is too free. It is clear that to speak about the slip of a knot is to repeat the thesis of foreclosure, since the Father function is situated as a knotting function in the schema of the Borromean knot.

What justifies this thesis? As I have already shown, it is supported by two pieces of data: on the one hand, Joyce's relation to his own body; and on the other, the nature of his writing. Two apparently very different phenomena that, nonetheless, are convergent signs, with the value of symptoms in the ordinary sense of the term.

The Imaginary in default

One of the three consistencies of the Borromean knot, the Imaginary, as Lacan called it, is not the imagination, nor is it reducible to a taste for images, nor even to the relationship between fellow human beings, who were not lacking for Joyce. Lacan said it again and again: it is the body. We recall the famous mirror stage where he asserted that the image, the form of one's own body, is the first object of libidinal investment, the first that lends itself to identification, wherein the little subject recognises himself for the first time, although hardly the last, since the speaking being remains, as Lacan puts it, 'infatuated' with his image. It is for each one the kernel of his ego. The violent affects associated with attacks on this form, whether intended or accidental, are testimony to this, as is the discomfort caused by malformations in others. In general, the ego's bodily anchorage explains many of the passions we therefore call imaginary. And who among us, when someone steps on our toes, has not experienced rage, indignation, dejection. Whatever the feeling, we are anything but indifferent, as if touching our body touches our very self. Indeed, it is the body that is involved in the most common passions: amorous conquests, ambition-driven competition, hateful fighting. This does not mean that affects come from the body. Rather, they come from the incorporated, linguistic unconscious; but without the body they do not exist.

Now Lacan has highlighted a phenomenon to which Joyce himself testified with respect to Stephen, apparently a quite subtle phenomenon, considered to be very rare, but not secondary, based on analytic experience. It has to do with an episode about the beating received by the main character of *Portrait of the Artist as a Young Man*. It is useless here to invoke standard ideas from literary criticism regarding the distinction between an author and his character, for from whom would the author take this phenomenon if not from himself, given that it is by no means common and cannot simply be imagined. The story tells of a young boy who is thrashed by his mates for not having yielded in a literary argument. After the episode, he realises that his anger vanishes rather than boils, as would have been normal for someone who would love his body as himself. Lacan says this is because 'the idea of the self, the self as body, carries weight. This is what is called the Ego' (S, p. 129). For the psychoanalyst, 'the form that this dropping of the relationship with the body takes for Joyce, is however, altogether suspicious'. In the relation to the body, the norm is that 'something of the psyche is affected, that it reacts, and that it is not detached' (ibid.) Detached from what, if not from the subject who is affected by it. Joyce, on the contrary, describes this body being 'dropped like a fruit peel' (S, p. 123). Only Lacan could have picked up on this trait, which is certainly pronounced but so discreetly that it takes up just a few lines. In any case, once this trait has been singled out, many other indications confirm what he designates as the 'slip of the knot', that is, an Imaginary unknotted from the Real and the Symbolic.

1/ Knot of the unknotted Imaginary

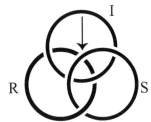

Joyce himself was quite explicit regarding his more generalised deficiency in the register of the passions, what Kant would call the register of the pathological, and he was astonished by it. Noting his own lack of vindictiveness after that episode he adds:

> [. . .] he wondered why he bore no malice now to those who had tormented him. He had not forgotten a whit of their cowardice and cruelty but the memory of it called forth no anger from him. All the description of fierce love and hatred which he had met in books had seemed to him therefore unreal. Even that night as he stumbled homewards along Jones's Road he had felt that some power was divesting him of that sudden woven anger as easily as a fruit is divested of its soft ripe peel.
>
> (*PAYM*, p. 62)

This same trait – the vanishing of any narcissistic vindictiveness, indicative of a certain peculiar relationship to the body as kernel of the ego – is seen again when he recounts a story, not of defeat, but of success in the theater. He who had noted about Stephen that he was 'different from others' (PAYM, p. 48) also described the moment of stepping onstage for a theatrical performance: 'Another nature seemed to have been lent him [. . .] for one rare moment he seemed to be clothed in the real apparel of boyhood' (p. 64). Soon afterwards, this very same person declares: 'A power, akin to that which had often made anger or resentment fall from him, brought his steps to rest' (PAYM, p. 65).

The disappearance of his rage following his beating by comrades, together with the inconsistency of his vanity after his theatrical success, can be linked with yet another, very insistent assertion: his indifference to his counterparts. Indeed, the ego's narcissism, the basis for many battles, always goes hand in hand with its opposite, the possibility for imaginary empathy with one's fellows. In contrast, Joyce – through Stephen – testifies to a bizarre detachment: '[his] ineradicable egoism which he was afterwards to call redeemer' which went all the way to a hatred for those around him (SH, p. 34). He himself emphasises its rarity, describing the main character as separated by an 'abyss' from the members of his family. 'No life or youth stirred in him as it had stirred in them. He had known neither the pleasure of companionship with others nor the vigor of rude male health nor filial piety. Nothing stirred within his soul but a cold and cruel and loveless lust' (PAYM, pp. 72–23). We are not, then, surprised that Joyce lends the following interpretation to Stephen's mother upon his departure from home: 'She prays now, she says, that I may learn in my own life and away from home and friends what the heart is and what it feels. Amen. So be it' (PAYM, p. 196).

This ferocious irony speaks to us of a being closed to pity, the foremost of the imaginary passions, and closed as well to sympathy and compassion. He is thus a being who pays no heed to the contagion of social affects. Is this not the portrait of a soul estranged from all imaginary participation with his fellows, whose 'mind . . . shone coldly on their strifes and happiness and regrets like a moon upon a younger earth'? (PAYM, p. 72).

A soul sheltered from the specular passions who mostly observes the world with the eyes of what I would call . . . an entomologist. Indirect confirmation: he carefully notes as rare occurrences two instances when Stephen was open to ordinary human affect. Once he had the satisfaction of experiencing some slight pity for a comrade; and once, after his famous lecture on a comment by a comrade, he perceived in himself a mild feeling of hope, so exceptional for him as to be worth noting.

To have a body

This slip of the knot, if one accepts it, requires that we question, in the case of Joyce, what we generally call narcissism, the love of self that is so vulnerable and often asserts itself so combatively. Clearly this is not lacking in Joyce. Did he not speak of a proud, 'impossible' certainty that had always 'made him conceive himself as a being apart in every order' (PAYM, p. 124), to envision 'converging to him the deeds and thoughts of his microcosm' (SH, p. 34), to make himself the herald of an art which would house the virulence of the drives that his mind's coldness did not exclude. How, then, for this detached individual, an unbeliever on top of it, one who does not consent to the Other – how then would he not be inclined to haughtiness and irony, to contemptuous regard for whatever lets itself be led by common passions, for anything that panders to the semblants of family, religion, politics, the couple itself? A dwelling, therefore, in 'silence, exile, and cunning' (PAYM, p. 191). The opposite of a militant, yes, but not the opposite of 'narcynicism', a narcissism whose sole cause is oneself, as I like to put it. Based on this, Lacan is quite right, Joyce was not a saint. He had too much pride in his art (*argueil*) (J/L, p. 33). Hence it is his art that one must interrogate, as Lacan does in his second lecture, where he also asks if it is necessary 'to maintain that man has a body, that is, that he speaks with his body' (p. 32) and asks if Joyce made his art speak with his body or not.

'*LOM* has a body' (ibid.). The being who speaks has a body, he is not a body. But what does it mean to have a body? Lacan could say of some people that they do not have a body. It was his new diagnosis, which he called the 'malady of mentality'. We understand that the expression is not to be taken in the sense of a simplistic realism, where the body is an image, the organism's form that can be photographed. We have photos of Joyce; he was neither phantom nor pure spirit. That man has a body means that he is able to make use of it, 'to do something with it' (ibid.) But it also means that he can suspend this power. When he uses it as an instrument at his disposal, then he will make of it, for example, a stepladder to promote his name in the Olympic Games. Or, in another configuration, he himself does not 'support' his body but makes others do it, making them pay their tithe, as in the case of mendicant brothers; and . . . on the side of women, through the erotic use of the body. Thus we say 'without a body' of someone who does not make use of it, does not engage it in the business of narcissistic sublimation. Conversely, someone who does engage in this engages more than an image. He engages the real of his jouissance symptom as 'body event' (Aé, p. 573) that owes nothing to the truth of speech and sometimes even shows itself 'in contradiction to anything likely to be true' for this being that is a *parlêtre* (language-being), made of words but who *has* a body.

According to Lacan, Joyce was 'cheap' (J/L, p. 33) with his body. This is another way of saying that he let his own body fall. If one does the opposite – sells it dearly – then it has many uses within the social link: for service, for the erotic, for promotion, all of which confirm just how much the libidinised body-image is constitutive of the ego. This body can therefore not be reduced to the specular image, nor to the sack that it is, for it is a sack with holes, libidinised by the operation of the Symbolic, provided Imaginary and Symbolic are knotted together in what we call the erogenous zones. But as a consequence of this – I stress this point – the *parlêtre* must also *a-ttribute* it to himself, this body that he has. The word evokes both the *a* and the *tribute*. The tribute – also called castration – that one has to pay to appropriate one's body, in order to be able to use it as an instrument in the social link. Well, this power is what Joyce instead suspended, set aside.

To shed light on Joyce's singularity, Lacan went to the trouble of once more clarifying two other uses of the body, those erotic uses that constitute the symptoms known as *woman* and as *hysteric* on the plane of the sexual couple. Two distinct types of 'body events'. From the beginning, Lacan had postulated the effect of *push-to-the-woman* produced by foreclosure, so perfectly illustrated by Freud's Schreber case. After asking whether Joyce believed himself to be a saviour, he could also question a possible feminisation of Joyce. A body can, indeed, be a symptom for another body, that is, a jouissance event for that other body. According to Lacan, in the sexual couple, this is the case for *a* woman. I want to add that this is not be understood in terms of anatomy alone, but has to do with whoever has the woman symptom in the relation between the sexes, she who lends herself to be a symptom, a body symptom, an event of jouissance for another body. She *is* symptom, which has nothing to do with the other symptoms she has. This is not the case for the hysteric, male or female, who puts the body on strike and delegates the symptom function of jouissance to a body that is not his or her own. Hence the trio, in which the hysteric places himself or herself as a third and does not offer his or her own body, but instead takes an interest in the jouissance between a body and the body of the symptom partner. Clinical illustrations abound, but I will not go into them.

Joyce is neither a hysteric nor a woman, for he does not use his body either to offer it or to provoke desire by withholding it. What he wanted, according to Lacan, was something else, 'to have nothing other than the stepladder of magisterial saying' (J/L, p. 33). He thus has nothing in common with *a* woman 'except to accomplish himself as a symptom' (p. 35). To accomplish: the term connotes striving, effort. *To accomplish* is already more than *to be* a symptom. It consists in wanting to be it. But this is not the *push-to-the-woman* symptom. Joyce does not offer his body. He does not make it into a *stepladder-sinthome*. Nor does he do this with any other body; this was not the function of his Nora.

It was not by making use of his body that Joyce coped with the slip of the knot. We can discern several other discrete signs of his setting the body aside. For example, his description of Stephen in *Portrait*, which is striking in this respect. Stanislaus, too, had noted it, inasmuch as it portrays a being who is puny, introverted, often numb, unwilling to engage in boyish brutalities, seeking shelter from these body-to-body skirmishes, seemingly quite different from how the young James had been. We can, of course, suppose that the romantic image of the artist was pushing in this direction, but this *topos* does not completely explain the contrast with the person his family called 'sunny James' for his gaiety, whose physical resistance and unfailing vitality impressed many a witness beyond his brother. We must also, I believe, take into consideration the very real way he treated his body, as testified to, over the course of his life, by episodes of insomnia and alcoholism, his interminable walkabouts and all manner of negligence, reported by his brother and also by his biographer. Most notably, his first stay in Paris, before Nora, when, having refused any possibility of working, he allowed himself to reach extremes of poverty, hunger and cold. So many signs that confirm that he is not . . . a somatology but a symptomatology. By not involving the body, he reveals, he illustrates, in all senses of the word, the very function of the symptom.

Without the unconscious

Thus Joyce brings our attention back to the connection between body and language, between Imaginary and Symbolic, since it is this latter that makes the body 'by incorporating itself in it' (Lacan, 1970, p. 61). Hence the notion of the 'civilized body' that I have sometimes used. For Joyce, his body that is not used as a stepladder goes hand in hand with the peculiarities of his relationship to language. I have already evoked his sensitivity to the heteronomy of the Symbolic and his refusal of the discourse of the Other. But there is more: to use his own word, the *'unusual'* nature of the relationship to *lalangue* that he attributes to the young Stephen. His taste for words, for rhythms, for the throbbing of linguistic matter, are testimony that, from the outset, he approaches *lalangue* as an object, an object that is disjoined from saying, separated from the functions of communication, working independently of what discourse transmits as meaning. It is indeed generally the opposite: discourse makes us forget or obstructs the vehicle which is *lalangue*. The number of passages Joyce devoted to this object is in itself revealing. The hypertrophy of the verbal thing and the exclusivity of *lalangue* are clearly related to failure of narcissistic identification via one's own body that in most cases governs what we call 'common sense'.

Joyce's singularity in this respect is manifest. Usually, language elaborated by discourse supplants *maternal lalangue*. It covers it with syntax and significations, the learning of which is, moreover, a *'de-maternalization'*, for 'one learns to read by making oneself alphabetically stupid' (Aé, p. 504). From then on, each of us is captive to a discourse that makes us forget *lalangue*, which nevertheless constitutes the real unconscious, where the verbal thing is enjoyed outside meaning. For Joyce, however, *lalangue* is laid bare due to his rejection of discourse, except, as we shall see, that it is not *his lalangue*, the one constitutive of his unconscious and of his fundamental symptom.

There we have it: Stephen Dedalus, a subject, the main character of *Stephen Hero* and of *Portrait*: captivated by words, he builds a 'thesaurus' for himself, his 'treasure' (the very term Lacan uses to designate the place of the Other), makes a 'garner' of words, wants to rescue them 'once for all' (SH, p. 26). And especially, he reads dictionaries, those works that, indeed, are not to be read, for they say nothing. The young man delights in them, fully occupied by the inventory of interconnections, derivations, infinite diffractions of meaning that destroy meaning. He thus becomes a 'poet with malice aforethought' who wants 'to explore the language for himself' (ibid.).

To this strange claim – that he is the agent of his own language instead of receiving it from the Other – is added another. The young Stephen, portrayed as a subject . . . listening, 'hypnotized by the most commonplace conversations' (ibid.). Tuned in, not to hallucinated voices, but to the voices of reality – all of which, close by or faraway, unimportant or convincing – are heard detached from their meaning, lending themselves to signifying the ineffable. Indeed, this barely audible murmuring transforms itself into epiphany.[1] What is banal becomes worthy of admiration, 'saving' words that demand to be interpreted. Is this not unique, this clamour of words, words so alive as to yearn for interpretation?

His emotions and his interests are thus directed much more toward words than toward people, a phenomenon that provides a counterweight to the failure of imaginary passions I mentioned above. Nothing can affect him more violently than the use of language. 'Unbounded contempt', 'intemperate anger', rage, enthusiasm, love, the entire boiling cauldron is addressed not to his fellows but to the manner in which they treat the verbal thing. The misuse of a term, a usage that is off, an instance of ignorance, immediately take on the value of a capital crime; and any flippancy regarding words is, in his eyes, a veritable degradation of life. We may surely ask what, in this singular relationship to speech, was imposed upon him. This is difficult to assess, since for him it is in the writing that 'speech is decomposed by imposing itself as such' (S, p. 79). Someone who scrutinises language 'not word by word but letter by letter' (SH, p. 32), who repeats expressions until they lose their significance and transform themselves into what, for him, are 'admirable words': is he not the martyr of a disorder that occurs 'at the innermost juncture of the subject's sense' not of life, as Lacan said about psychosis (É, p. 466), but of assent? The assent brought about by any signifier once perceived, that gives it its suggestive power. Indeed, in the pages just mentioned, Joyce quotes from *Grammar of Assent* by John Henry Newman. In this refusal of assent, do we not again find 'the unfathomable decision of being' (É, p. 145)?

'*Without the unconscious*'. With these words, I am only articulating Lacan's thesis, which says that Joyce 'cancelled his subscription to the unconscious' (J/L, p. 26). Something strange for one who subscribed to the pulverised equivocations of *lalangue* that form the unconscious. But in Joyce, that specialist of the pure letter outside meaning, we have to speak instead of the interweaving of languages with which he plays, to unmake common language and make it *his* language. This will be an occasion for us to clarify the status of the unconscious.

If it is structured like a language and deciphered, the unconscious – no matter how we define it – is read. According to Lacan, even analysands can learn to read it. But what is it that we read? In psychoanalysis, Freud was the first teacher. From him, we learned to read the analysand's speech for 'what it says': the meaning, the meaning of desire. Freud called this desire unconscious and indestructible, the unique and constant signified of unconscious productions. We read desire, but not without deciphering it in speech, word by word, the words of the drive and of jouissance. At the beginning, Lacan followed Freud regarding the unconscious subject, before advancing further. He conceived the unconscious as structured like a language, that is, as a signifying chain which, to be sure, signifies desire and its lack, but more than that – for signs cipher – jouissance. One more step brought him to recognising *lalangue* as the place, the site of unconscious knowledge, knowledge that is spoken and enjoyed. This is different from the signifier of desire. Unconscious language is a '*motérialité*' rather than a signifying chain. By this measure, we cannot say whether, for the psychoanalyst, Joyce is more of an ally or an *alien*. In *Finnegans Wake* at least, '*motérialité*' is apparently all he knows. Should we say he subscribes to *lalangue*? Well, no, for it is not *lalangue*, neither his nor ours. It is languages, their equivocations made to sparkle seductively through the writing, to the point of point of ab-sense. Uninterpretable as to meaning, then? Even unreadable? Rather, 'not-to-be-read' if one believes Lacan, who says that writing is not to read, that is to say, not to be interpreted, and he says this of his own *Écrits*. Why 'not-to-be-read'? Isn't this because the letters of the writing carry not meaning but jouissance? They are real. And Lacan adds about this 'not-to-be-read': 'This was established well before my discoveries since, after all, it was Joyce who introduced writing as not-to-be-read. To put it better: he *intra-traduced* it. For, in doing word trade beyond languages, he hardly every translates, to make it everywhere equally unreadable' (Aé, p. 504).

A real find, this phrase 'word trade' – just as one says 'slave trade' – a trade in languages, one for another. It points to the fact that the *lalangue* which the young Stephen *exposed* (as I like to put it), a language by means of which he rid himself of the hated traces of common language, helped for sure by the enormous body of literature he so passionately assimilated during the whole of his childhood, this language was not *his*, in the sense of *his* unconscious. The unconscious is made from maternal *lalangue*, which constitutes the original bath for every newborn. But this maternal language is already itself a subtraction from language, for each mother speaks *her* language, with its words, incarnated words that carry meaning for her, but also a weight of jouissance particular to them. From this set, the child will receive only those that he himself has invested with meaning and jouissance. As I said earlier, a language is the integral of its equivocations, but an unconscious is nothing but the sum of the jouissance letters that belong to a *parlêtre* (*speaking being*), precisely those that are incarnated for him. In the end, the language-unconscious is the enjoyed letter.

It is not an exaggeration to say that each of us has his or her *lalangue*, another name for the unconscious: the one that marks his or her body and inscribes there both the drives and the letter of the fundamental symptom. On this point, Joyce differs from everyone else with a language beyond languages, whose letters are, for him, manifestly a jouissance object, a jouissance of the letter that is felt. But this body of enjoyed letters fabricated from a multiplicity of languages, an ever-expanding body, is not an incorporated *lalangue*. Hence the extraordinary freedom of equivocations, the puns so specific to Joyce, a playing with the body of a *lalangue* that is hardly carnal. This exposure of the jouissive *motérialité* of the Word thus reveals the very essence of the symptom. But it comes at the price of a denunciation of every language that is concrete and particular, including that of his family, his so-called race, and the invading British Empire. 'He is the pure symptom of what is involved in the relationship to language' (J/L, p. 27), language in general. Hence, it is not only from the unconscious as producer of meaning that Joyce cancels his subscription, but also from the anchorage in the maternal *lalangue* that usually constitutes the knot of the symptom, insofar as the symptom makes 'the unconscious exist' outside the Symbolic in the Real, as Lacan says in *R.S.I.*

Without a woman

I am taking a risk with this paradoxical formula, 'without a woman'. How can one say this about a man for whom the unique Nora was so clearly essential, if not vital? Joyce of course never said this, which leaves the 'fact' pending. To be sure, there are the love letters, but they say something else, namely that this person without body was not at all deprived of the jouissance called perverse, to which the partial drives give form. Freud noted this from the start, hence the notion of jouissance as generalised perversion. Joyce never said Nora was crucial to him, but he demonstrated it by his behaviour and, in the end, with a gesture, when finally he married her, contradicting the programme he had articulated when he asserted he would never marry. We cannot really call it an act, after all those years together, his age, his success . . .

Yet there is no doubt Nora was his chosen woman, the only one, in spite of two or three minor dalliances. Lacan says: 'For Joyce, there is but one woman' (S, p. 68). Indeed, something rather rare and about more than monogamy. When she wants to leave, he goes after her to bring her back. She was his, absolutely, everything shows it, but in what way? In the end, by some obscure harmony. Unconscious to unconscious, if I can put it like that. Nora never passed into the realm of lost objects. There are various ways to be attached to someone; the question cannot be answered at the level of observable reality. What is more conventional than a wife and children? Nevertheless, it says nothing about Joyce's heterosexuality or his actual position as a father, this *non-dupe* who is a stranger to any Oedipal solution. That he *is* symptom leaves open the question of knowing what symptom he *has* as complement to the body, and what is his own sexual position.

Lacan posed this question at the precise moment in his teaching when his concept of what founds sexual identity was no longer the same as it was at the beginning, with his return to Freud and to the Freudian Oedipus. We will see the importance of the theoretical reversal he accomplished if, right away, I emphasise that he ceased to believe in what he had maintained for years on end until *L'étourdit*, in 1972, namely that identification to anatomical sex depends on the function of the father and on the couple of the paternal metaphor. This topic is a matter of debate among readers of Lacan and clearly has consequences for any thesis about the sexuation of the psychotic subject.

a-normal-ity

According to Freud, the purpose of the Oedipus complex was to assure transmission of the Law against incest and, on this basis, produce effects on the level of sexual identification. In accordance with anatomical sex, the child would become either a man or woman along the pathways of heterosexual normality that conditions reproduction. The Oedipal father thus has a normalising function that is at once social and sexuating. The paternal metaphor, with which Lacan rewrote the Oedipus in a linguistic version that marked its determination by the Symbolic, changed nothing of this sexuating function. Numerous texts leave no doubt about this.[2] It follows that, in psychosis, foreclosure of the Name of the Father can only translate to a deficiency in virility; and this is what Lacan illustrates with Freud's Schreber case. With the paternal metaphor, the alternative *man/woman* is reformulated as the phallic alternative *having/ being*. Schreber, because he did not see himself as having the phallic attribute within the metaphor, was condemned to be it, under the form of *push-to-the-woman*.

But Lacan rejected his own advances, first and foremost, the sexuating function of the metaphor – and he did so categorically. It is often emphasised that he moved to the plural, the Names of the father, and then to the Father of the Name. But it is not so much these formulations that challenge the metaphor. There is another one that shakes it to its very foundations: 'there is no sexual rapport.' (Aé, p. 413). But there are, after all, relations between the sexes and also within each of us; so we need to say how these are established. Lacan's final thesis on this point is that they are constructed by means of the unconscious, like any symptom. This is why he finished by saying that, for a man, a woman is a symptom. But a symptom is always singular, one by one. As for symptoms that make up for the absence of the sexual rapport – symptoms capable of producing a relation to a partner, man or woman – there are many and various.

The thesis of a symptom that functions as supplementation to the foreclosure of the sexual relation – this is a thesis that Lacan established in disagreement with himself. It is in disagreement with his own metaphor of the man-father as agent of the sexual discourse in relation to his other, his wife-mother, the metaphor that makes him, let us say, the master of order, if not in the house, at least, in the bedroom. And, in contradistinction to the comments he made about Little Hans in *La Relation d'objet* where he had been seeking the motive for Hans' phobia, he bluntly formulates that what Hans lacked was a father who 'fucks the mother'. Why not also a mother who lets herself be laid? It would be more in line with what we know about the family and what Hans also knew. In 'The Agency of the Letter in the Unconscious', Lacan plainly speaks about the sexual disunion of Hans' parents as the 'failings of his symbolic entourage' at the moment when 'the suddenly actualised enigma to him of his sex and his existence, develops' (É, p. 432). This says – categorically – that the Symbolic of the metaphor orders the sexual. We can also hear this in Winnicott's 'breakfast father', evoked as such because it gives us the idea that he spent the night in the mother's bedroom. But Lacan himself changed his mind. I quote: 'The analyst is just as liable as anyone else to have a bias regarding sex, above and beyond what the unconscious reveals to him' (É, p. 615). In any case, an appeal to the fathers referenced above is surely in clear contradiction to everything that follows, both theoretically and in practice, regarding the sexual non-rapport, as well as to what we currently observe as the effect of capitalism.

So what about Joyce? Is it any surprise that Lacan asked if Joyce thought himself a woman after having asked if he took himself to be a saviour? These are questions that attempt to situate the repercussions of '*de facto* foreclosure', which he had diagnosed, and which is a foreclosure in addition to that of the sexual relation. Lacan concluded in the negative, once he recalled that a woman 'is a symptom of another body' (J/L, p. 35). Joyce was not a symptom for another body; he is just a symptom, indeed, a symptomatology, and succeeds as such. However, to do this, it was not enough for him to write; he needed to publish. In doing so, indeed he offered himself for feeding upon, the way a woman does. But here is the difference: he offered himself to the vast, skinless body of his many readers, the so-called Joyceans, who made of him the artist he wanted to be. What he offered was not his fleshly body but his body of words, his wit, what he called the 'book of himself' (S, p. 56). What, then, could he make of a woman?

The woman who is of no use

How can we situate the indubitable strength of Joyce's relation to Nora? The paradox of 'without a woman' that I used above is resolved only if we are clear about what it means, according to Lacan, for a man to have a woman that he can call his own. This is related to analytic experience ever since Freud described the various types of object choice – not just one – and Lacan, for his part, posited that, in the absence of the sexual rapport, the choice of sexed partner – specifically a man's choice of a woman – obeys conditions specific to him and that are always a function of the unconscious. For a man with the *father version* of the symptom, his partner is defined as follows: *a* woman he views as his (this does not mean she is his only woman or that they have married) and whom he acquires to give him children. We can be sure that Nora was other than this, as Joyce himself is other.

Ever since Freud, we have known about the narcissistic relation to the partner. However, there is nothing like that with Nora. Those close to Joyce were surprised by this disparate choice of a woman so remarkably uncultivated, so dissimilar to him. She was hardly acquired on the basis of intellectual affinities; nor was she a mother in the Freudian schema. She did not take care of her body, or of her bodily comfort, never prepared their meals, even in the direst of circumstances dining daily at the restaurant. This choice is neither narcissistic nor anaclitic. Should we assume that erotic benefits were primary? It does not seem to be the case. Lacan's firm hypothesis was that '. . . he only slips on this glove with the keenest repugnance' (S, p. 68). A very strong word, 'repugnance'. There were, yes, erotic letters from Joyce to Nora. But erotic letters do not involve body to body. On the contrary, a separation of bodies; and this precisely is what gives free range to the phantasy and to the letter. Eroticism, scatological and masturbatory, is obvious in them, whereas Nora's role is not particularly clear. And, based on some reports, matters – when Joyce was home – were quite unlike those ardent letters. Nor was Nora acquired to make children; each child was the occasion for a major drama. We know that Joyce did not officially record Giorgio's birth until one year later and only because he was required to do so. In addition, he was given the name of a dead brother. . . . Contrary to what happens in the case of the *father symptom*, as Lacan noted, children were not part of the plan. In other words, children were not written into a symptomatic programme that moreover had no link to Nora, nor were they part of the specific bond that tied him to her. Here perhaps is some subtle link to their future destinies, Lucia's schizophrenia, Giorgio's severe alcoholism. Everything indicates that their births were a problem for Joyce and that he could not bear the change motherhood produced in Nora. In a letter he wrote to his aunt following the birth of the eldest, Giorgio, he notes the change in their relationship and the abandonment he suffers: 'I am not a very domestic animal – after all, I suppose, I am an artist' (SL, p. 81). Yet while he complains bitterly about the birth of his children, he does not abandon them. He encouraged and protected them, doing everything in his power so Giorgio could become a tenor, in accordance with family tradition. As for Lucia, he fiercely protected her as long as possible against the psychiatrists.

So, what about Nora? Lacan's answer: she serves no purpose. 'It is quite tangible that he made Nora his chosen woman only by virtue of the strongest depreciation' (S, p. 68). The word 'depreciation' merits an explanation. It seems to contradict all evidence we have of Joyce's actual esteem for Nora and the clear fact that he used her all his life. But, according to Lacan, when it comes to a woman, 'depreciation' does not mean the narcissistic diminution of a person's qualities. At a time when Lacan produced his thesis about a woman as symptom for a man, the term refers to her function as a woman, that is, a body involved in the jouissance of another body. Is this not precisely the symptom that serves the jouissance in which everyone is most interested, that is really the most valued, even if there is a cost to the ego?

Implicit in Lacan's statement is that appreciating a woman consists in elevating her to the rank of symptom, in other words, making use of her for jouissance. Such a thesis might appear off the mark in a time when the narcissistic demand for recognition and parity is at its height. There is a question here. Men and women can be equal in many ways, even completely equal in the realm of social reality. But does equality have meaning at the level of the erotic? Today, we know that some believe in this and campaign for it, but always at the price of a denial of the unconscious. Interestingly, Lacan – always so in tune with the times – does not indulge the era one bit on this point. Rather, he maintains that a woman as a man's symptom is based not on the equality of the sexes, but on their incommensurability in matters of jouissance.

Joyce, as someone who went beyond the prejudices of his time, was able to value Nora, her simplicity, her goodness, her rectitude, her flexibility and imagination. But he did not make her into a jouissance symptom, which would have been tantamount to appreciating her as *a* woman. His symptom is his writing, and to enjoy the letter and make from it a name for himself, he does not go through the body of Nora. That there is the exile of the sexual rapport – for him, as for everyone who speaks – makes it that much easier. Lacan, in the lesson of 13 January 1976, tells us that Joyce wrote *Exiles* under 'Nora's reign' and that it is 'really an approach to something that for him is the core symptom [. . .] which is formed from the specific shortcoming of the sexual rapport' (S, p. 56). It is true that the symptom is formed from the sexual non-rapport; and that sometimes it is the *père-version* (father-version). But for Joyce, on the contrary, the symptom just is 'that there is really no reason for him to hold one-woman-among-others to be *his* woman' (ibid.). Right from the start he told Nora she would never be his wife, that he would never marry her. So he would never say even an implicit 'you are my woman'. Indeed, if he did not think of himself as a man among others, how could he consider this woman to have been elected, unique, his own, in accordance with the standard Oedipal solution?

An egoistic prosthesis

This is why, correlatively, Lacan could add that Nora 'fits him like a glove' (S, p. 68), whereas the symptom, whatever its jouissance benefits, never fits like a glove. Rather it puts us at odds with ourselves and always includes the incommodious, irrepressible *dit-mention* of the unconscious. Besides, it is hardly a mystery that valorisation of a woman as symptom does not at all favour peace in the household. 'Like a glove': with this expression, Lacan accentuates the function of the Imaginary, while his definition of the symptom accentuates the knotting of Real and Symbolic.

The glove that grips and . . . holds tight. Lacan often used a reference he borrowed from Immanuel Kant, a reference to a glove that can be turned inside out to make the right-hand glove fit the left. The inside-out glove is of interest because it nullifies and, in doing so, reveals the dissymmetry inherent in the specular relation, which itself is manifest in the inversion of right and left in the mirror, showing that, in spite of appearance, the reflected image is not identical to its model. The turning inside out of the glove nullifies this difference (the right glove fits the left hand), except when the glove has a button, a case Kant neglected to consider. When this glove, the one with the button, is turned inside out, the outside button is now found inside. The difference between the subject and his specular image is restored! It is not surprising that Lacan connects this button with the clitoris and thus to phallic difference.

He notes that 'all that subsists of sexual rapport is the geometry to which we alluded with regard to the glove' (S, p. 70). This is true, not for Joyce but for everyone. This development is important because it completes the thesis of the symptom as function of the letter, $f(x)$. The jouissance of the letter of the unconscious, which puts it between Symbolic and Real, thus allows Lacan to state: 'We make love with our unconscious'. The geometry of the glove reintroduces the Imaginary of the body as something at play in the sexual act. But usually – there is the button.

The inside-out glove is Nora. But if she fits him like a glove, it is because there is no button. There has been a cancellation of the heterogeneity between subject and object, which even the mirror preserves, given that the image is the first object. The expression indicates a relation in which not only the *heteros*, the Other, is absent, but in which Imaginary difference itself is surmounted: no button on the glove. I will evoke here a kind of object transitivism, which perhaps was not reciprocal (we do not know what Joyce was for Nora), but which created for her some heavy responsibilities once she consented to them.

Surely Nora had to accept his debauched lifestyle, with the obligation for her to put up with his personality and alcoholism, his moodiness and decisions to move house. And above all, the obligation to focus on him and him alone, and to do this with the eye through which he saw himself, thus annulling the split between the eye and the gaze. This is what we hear in the letter mentioned above, in which Joyce complains about an eye that, at Giorgio's birth, no longer sees him as the artist. She did not really have the power of speech. This does not mean that she was gagged, but that what she says is of no importance. In Joyce, there is nothing like 'my wife says . . .' He is always the one with the determining say-so that derives not from what we call will, but from an existential certainty that nothing can deflect. My hypothesis: between Joyce and Nora, it is not so much the classic case, in which the phallic objection blocks the sexual rapport. It is, rather, what I will term the *egotistical* objection, equivocating here between *egotistical* and what makes up for it, that is, his *ego-symptom*. This is what prevented him from 'deifying' Nora as Other of the voice, the one he believed in. Nora was not Joyce's God. Instead, according to Lacan, it was during Nora's reign that the non-rapport – which is structural – was revealed to him. For most of us, it is veiled by the symptomatic relation, so much so that it requires the whole of the psychoanalytic elaboration to produce the thesis, a thesis not learned from books. For the reign of an adored one to unveil the non-rapport instead of the usual – covering it up at least for a time – one would have to be the *egotistical Joyce*. But 'he knew very well that his relations with women were his own unique song' (Lacan, 1989, p. 25).

What then remains of this relation, if this woman was neither a symptom nor the god of his life? My conclusion: a glove that annuls disparity. A strange sort of 'relationship', scarcely sexual, reduced to the geometry of the Imaginary envelope, a geometry normally knotted to the symptom of jouissance.

Elected unconditionally by Joyce, Nora is not for him the one-woman jouissance symptom. She in no way serves him in his posing as a man. In no way is she part of his phallic gear. She is not even named in his *sinthome*. At most, she is an Imaginary extra in Joyce's singular ego.

Thus my conclusion regarding Joyce's three negative, symptomatic singularities. They make plain the question of the subjective function of his work. For, if he has neither body, nor unconscious, nor a woman, he has an *Ego* and a name, forged by his work.

Notes

1 See 'Return to the Epiphanies' in Chapter 6 of this book.
2 See my conclusion.

Chapter 6

Borromean Art

In the unfolding of the seminar on Joyce – concerning his being as a supplementation sinthome – we can discern two layers in Lacan's demonstration. The first layer concerns the name Joyce gave to himself; the second concerns his art.

Without genealogy

There is, to begin with, a central thesis, revisited in various passages. The thesis makes the name Joyce gave himself, as illustrated in his work, a *supplementation sinthome* for the *de facto foreclosure*. In place of the assent he refused his father, Joyce wanted assent addressed to his own name. According to Lacan, he wanted his name to be paid 'a homage he refused to anyone else' (S, p. 73). This is a subjective choice, no doubt. It clearly presupposes that, beyond writing, there will be publication. But, as Lacan says, 'the proper noun is something strange in Joyce' (ibid.). Why? In what way has he done anything more than push an ambition for fame to the extreme? Well, it is strange that his name is what he 'valorizes at the expense of the father' (ibid.). This is not the usual case. On the contrary. Usually, when there is a 'de facto' father (to forge an expression modelled on *de facto foreclosure*), there will be sons or daughters who perpetuate the famous name that was acquired by hard work, accomplishments, even accomplishments in the field of love, 'those most engaging realities', as Lacan referred to them (Aé, p. 310). The name the children perpetuate will serve the family tree, make fathers proud, 'put god in a good mood' (ibid.).

But Joyce did not work for the family tree. Rather, he claims to abolish it, to make himself, paradoxically, the beginning, the origin. To cite the last words of *A Portrait of the Artist:* 'I go to encounter for the millionth time the reality of experience and to forge in the smithy of my soul the uncreated conscience of my race' (PAYM, p. 196). This 'I go', this is the moment when the *Nego*, expressed so many times in speech and intention, becomes act; the moment when, refusing reality to all experience predating his departure, he makes himself into a beginning, fashions himself, sublimates himself into a conscience born – not carnally from a father – but from his race. The replacement name he gives himself places him at the origin. But nomination, wherever it comes from, is inseparable from a social link. I have developed this theme elsewhere; there is no self-nomination, for even if one wants a name for oneself, nomination supposes assent from a partner. And Joyce, if he is an origin, is an origin of a series of Joyceans, readers occupied with him, and his public. In any case, Lacan added something which he demonstrated on the basis of the Borromean knot: it is that the name supports a 'corrective ego' which restores the Borromean knotting of the Imaginary.

2/ Knot of the unknotted Imaginary

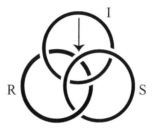

3/ Knot of the Corrective Ego

Thus a special ego, itself a replacement, made not from the stuff of the body, but from a name. And if there is something strange in his name, we must also add that there is something strange also in his *ego*, which is of a different nature than is usually the case. In what ways are the singularities of the artist's name and his ego articulated?

In the Borromean knot that knots the three consistencies, the ego is not the fourth that knots, but one of the three that is knotted, for it is specifically based on the Imaginary of the body with which everyone is infatuated. The ego's knot with the Symbolic renders it inseparable from meaning, produced between Imaginary and Symbolic. We can say that everyone enjoys meaning – *'joui-sens'* to quote Lacan – and everyone believes that it is shared with others, however partially, calling it 'common sense'. The singularity of Joyce's ego shows itself, as I have already emphasised, in his non-participation in the 'sense' said to be common, in his non-participation in shared beliefs and their accompanying passions, rivalries, emulations, rancours, and so forth. In general, we denounce these passions, but we must not fail to see that they allow each of us to recognise ourselves in others and are at the foundation of shared feelings and empathy. These are the passions that lead us to say 'let him who is without sin . . .'. But Joyce declares these passions to be something curiously foreign; and more than that, regards them with a hostility both ferocious and vigilant, if we are to believe Stanislaus. A strange *ego* that excludes the mirroring effects of relations with others and thus the shared complicity of Imaginary battles. The body of this *ego* is not a body Joyce *has*, but a body he gives himself, the body of 'the book of himself', the book he 'makes [himself] be', (S, p. 56), as I already said. And Lacan confirms that Joyce 'turns out to have targeted, in a privileged way, through his art, the fourth term known as the *sinthome*' (p. 27). 'How can an art target in an expressly divinatory way the substantialisation of the *sinthome*?' (p. 28). Yet in the seminar devoted to Joyce, this is the main question. For, more than just aiming at the *sinthome*, Joyce succeeded in making up for it, restoring a knotting of the three consistencies by renaming himself; and he did this by way of his very singular *ego*. As noted above, writing was not enough. There would also have to be publication. Lacan was curious about the reason for and the function of publishing *Finnegans Wake*, that text of autistic jouissance, as Lacan called it in *'Joyce le symptôme'*. But I realised that the seminar says more, namely that 'Joyce's text is fashioned just like a Borromean knot' (S, p. 132). There is something surprising here. In fact, in the Joyce of *Finnegans Wake*, Lacan had diagnosed a *literary symptom* that short circuits meaning by way of a special use of equivocation. How can a text that short circuits meaning – that therefore operates between Symbolic and Real without passing through the Imaginary – an art that confirms the unknotting of the Imaginary, how can such an art be Borromean?

The pulverulence of equivocations

We know that psychoanalysts in general are interested in the question of meaning, given that equivocation is their weapon against the symptom, at least insofar as they follow the Freudian practice of deciphering, with its dismantling of what he called condensation and displacement, theorised by Lacan in terms of language. He said it many times and he returned to it in the seminar on Joyce: the only thing the analyst has at his disposal, with any chance of moving the fixity of the symptom, is equivocation. The thesis had already been asserted in *L'étourdit:* interpretation produces its effect via equivocation. It is taken up again in *R.S.I.* and confirmed in *The Sinthome*. The paradox is that Joyce turns equivocation into his symptom, that is to say, his jouissance. There where analysis uses equivocation to unmake the symptomatic fixity of jouissance, to make it slide toward other signs or other *joui-senses*, Joyce goes in the opposite direction. He fixes jouissance in the very pulverulence of equivocation, in *lalangue* itself as an 'integral of the equivocations that its history permitted to persist there' (L'é, p. 47). With Joyce, the thing totally snowballs, since *Finnegans Wake* is not written in one language only, but in several; and it is this mixing of multi-linguistic equivocations that Joyce really enjoys.

In psychoanalysis, the use of equivocation has a precise aim. If we pretend that another word has been heard – competing with the lapsus – if we hear one signifier in place of another, if we dissemble and preach the false, it is to make another term appear, perhaps leading the One of the symptom to emerge from the chain wherein its jouissance has been metonymised; or conversely, to undo a fixation. Joyce, in contrast, is the one who makes the unconscious exist. To make the unconscious exist is to subtract the letter from the chain of meaning and fix therein a jouissance outside meaning. This is why Lacan could say that Joyce abolishes meaning. I believe Joyce would not have denied this. For, when Terence Gervais White asked him whether there was any meaning to be found, Joyce answered: 'No, it's pure music' and furthermore, 'No, no, it's meant to make you laugh' (Ellmann, 1982, p. 703). The only problem is that this manipulation of the sonorous letter makes enigma surge forth at each step; and enigma is the height of meaning. And for Joyce, enigma has a precise function, to which I will return.

Thus Joyce accentuates an aspect present in every symptom, for there is no symptom that is not an offence to sense, to meaning, to what we call 'common sense', 'good sense', the sense which allows us – more or less – to get along with our neighbour, recognise ourselves in him; the sense outside of which the madman dwells, the sense always regulated by discourse. Common sense has nothing natural about it. It is an effect of discourse, produced by the ordering of jouissances within a social link that is a given for any discourse. The secret of meaning is that it is always found on the side of jouissance. This is what psychoanalysis postulates. What we can deduce from this is that where we find common sense, we also find the seat of prejudice, and even the shaping of libidinal satisfactions.

In contrast, the symptom always objects to common sense because, in psychoanalysis, the meaning one gives to the neurotic or perverse symptom is always singular and is never a question of good sense. There is nothing commonsensical about the symptom. This is why the neurotic – who is not at all mad – with his symptom nevertheless 'unsubscribes' from common sense. Joyce, however, goes much further. Lacan says: 'cancels his subscription to the unconscious' (S, p. 144), to mark the difference from neurosis. Not only does he not turn to the commonplace, he is supremely indifferent to the question that torments the neurotic: 'what does this mean?'. But more than that, he does not resort to the private *lalangue* that for each speaking being [*parlêtre*] fixes his jouissance; rather, he resorts to a mix of languages and written letters. This is a voluntary cancellation and a conscious one. In *Stephen Hero*, Joyce makes the young Stephen articulate what he abhors: 'He was determined to fight with every energy of soul and body against any possible consignment to what he now regarded as the hell of hells – the region, otherwise expressed, wherein everything is found to be obvious . . .' (*SH*, p. 30).

This methodical, calculated anti-Cartesianism applies to Joyce himself. For the commonplace – so consubstantial with good sense, so necessary for thinking like one's neighbour, for repeating over and over the same refrain – is this not for Joyce the worst possible thing? And when the young Stephen takes a firm decision to launch himself into a career of letters, so sure of his own hatred and profound disgust for everything that people agree upon or that causes consensus, is this not close enough to what we know of James, to be able to consider Stephen to be his spokesman? It is hardly a matter of indifference that this statement occurs in the passage where Joyce, that great reader of dictionaries, evokes his 'treasure', words and language; and where he describes a hero hypnotised by the most banal conversations, which he elevates to the level of admirable epiphanies. It is a of way of saying that he manages to imbue them with a value quite foreign to their common meaning.

If we are to believe Jacques Lacan, Joyce – with his handling of equivocations in *Finnegans Wake* – establishes himself as a master of the unreadable. The love letters enchant, for they offer up love's meaning for the jouissance of the reader. The unreadable letters astonish, in the strong sense of the term as used by Descartes, for whom astonishment is the foremost passion, correlated to the encounter with a new object. What I want to posit first is that one cannot choose to be unreadable, echoing Lacan who often noted that 'one cannot choose to go crazy'. One can always ask: unreadable for how long? Moreover, not everything unreadable is the same. There can be false unreadables. Sometimes we call 'unreadable' what is unintelligible because it is too new, too much a precursor in terms of its form or of its substance. Was this not precisely Lacan's case? Over the course of a period of ten years, he said, there was a progressive passage to intelligibility.

The truly unreadable, even when explained, remains unreadable, and resists assimilation. Take, for example Raymond Roussel. No matter how much trouble he took to explain his 'How to do', his manufacturing secrets and rules to be followed, his text remains unreadable. In general, according to Lacan, the truly written is not to be read. This is because the operation of reading is not about deciphering letters; it is always about giving them meaning. Reading, therefore, is an operation that presupposes the Borromean anchoring of signifying chains. There needs to be a knotting of Imaginary and Symbolic out of which meaning arises and from which the real of the letter beyond meaning is shut out. To summarise, Joyce's use of language is most unusual. His way of playing with words certainly lends itself to being confused with mechanisms of the unconscious, but only in appearance. In reality, it puts it outside the domain of witticism or lapsus. The witticism is also a play on words, but one which stops after making – to our great pleasure – a bit of sense emerges from nonsense. As for the lapsus, which gets the signifier wrong, it is open to interpretation only because it is not open to just any meaning. Its error was in the service of a precise satisfaction, called *Befriedigung* by Freud, always circumscribed, always specific to the subject. Joyce pushes the game to its limits, to the point where, as children say, it is not fun anymore. His writing crosses the barrier beyond which there is only the materiality of a letter, whose handling is no longer limited by the purposes of *joui-sens* and which thus retains only a meaning that is pulverised, uninterpretable. This is what had already impressed Jung, reading *Ulysses*, and it would also be of interest to Lacan and to every psychoanalyst: Joyce, the uninterpretable.

The dispute between psychoanalyst and literary critic is focused on this point. The latter seems to find meaning everywhere, whereas the former maintains there is none. Both are correct, but from diametrically opposed perspectives. The meaning that interests the psychoanalyst is not just any meaning: it is the meaning which – because simultaneously circumscribed and demanded by the *joui-sens* of speaker or author – permits one to interpret the subject supposed to the text. In contrast, in *Finnegans Wake* meaning glitters in the material-letter and its innumerable knots, so pulverised, as I have said, as to be reduced to enigma. The reader is entirely in charge of specifying it and is made into an interpreter, but with risks. Because it is the reader, through his or her own reading, who is being interpreted. The author remains outside. This is so because in the end, the jouissance of Joyce the artist seems more akin to that of a mathematician than of a novelist, since the mathematician, like the calligrapher, also in his own way short-circuits meaning.

Unreadable letters

Here we seem to encounter another of Joyce's particularities: a progressive unreadability. But is this really true? Certainly, if Joyce became unreadable, he was not always so. He established himself first as readable – scandalous, perhaps, this is always relative – but readable. In no way can we put *Chamber Music, Dubliners, Stephen Hero, A Portrait of the Artist* on the side of unreadability. One could reasonably think that his *work in progress* is a culmination, a metamorphosis of a writing that methodically and progressively opts out of a literature of meaning, with *Ulysses* constituting the major turning point.

Nonetheless, I believe that, upon careful inspection, what presents itself as an evolution was in fact there from the beginning. Between the readable poems of his youth and the strange epiphanies from the same period, there is approximately the same relation as between *Portrait* and *Finnegans Wake*: it is the difference between the readable and the enigmatic. Primarily from his correspondence with Stanislaus, we know how intensely Joyce valued those deposits of language that are the epiphanies, and with what certainty he identified them with his calling and his future work. However one considers them, these epiphanies are enigmas to the reader; the question of their meaning is unsettled. Thus, from readable to unreadable, there is not diachrony but synchrony. From the beginning, the epiphanic process attacks the coherence of situations and of discourse. Down with the obvious! This was the first manifestation of a methodical enterprise of dissolving semblance that culminates in *Finnegans Wake* and defines precisely what I am calling the true unreadable: a text which paradoxically 'ex-ists' to the Symbolic, and is therefore homologous to what is most real in the symptom.

Finnegans Wake is a massacre of signifyingness, if one defines this as the use of words appropriate to representing the subject of interpretation. It is not that one cannot give a meaning to the text. It is that one can give a multiplicity of meanings, none of which will be more likely than any other to represent the text's subject. Open to all meanings, the text becomes uninterpretable, for readability, while it is never univocal, nonetheless implies that the meaning is limited. But here, all moorings of legibility are broken, and first of all of these, the narrative vector characteristic of a novel. There are, of course, names, characters, figures, the whole 'chaosmos' as Umberto Eco puts it, even a pseudo-theme, *the Fall*. But there is no storyline, no narrative timeframe. On the contrary, there is a closed circuit of narrative whose unresolved ending leads back to the beginning. 'Riverun', the first word, receives its article only with the last word, 'the', looping it back and capsizing the irreversible linearity of the storyline.

Here equivocation – never eliminable from language – crosses the barrier of misunderstanding that psychoanalysis operates with in its practice. The pulverulence of polysignifyingness is stopped by nothing and diffracts, to the point of infinity, the linguistic crystal. From this text that appears to be beyond the saying, an erudite scholar can make anything he or she wants, without managing either to interpret or to contradict it. Proof by the negative, as I have said: when Lacan pastiches Joyce, he never equals him, never attains the Joycean level of freedom which, it seems, seeks to explore the entirety of the equivocations of *lalangue*. But even this is not enough, for this *lalangue* is multiplied tenfold by the polyglot, translingual amalgam of some sixty-five languages that Joyce plays with, producing in the end a subversion of lexicon, grammar, syntax and narrativity. The result is that neither metaphor nor metonymy work here; and the text, bearing no message, in effect forecloses truth, just as science does, except that the Joycean text still evokes it, but as elusive enigma.

This writing goes all the way to knocking over 'the stepladder' of poetic speech, even though Joyce himself had certainly once made forays into this. As Lacan noted, poetry could well be the 'least stupid saying', the least likely of any to fall into readymade grooves. Whatever its art of the letter, it remains within the order of saying, that is, the readable. The poet, like the prophet of former times, produces a new discourse that reorders the foundation for common significations. Joyce is neither of these. From *Ulysses* on, Joyce hit home in terms of the structural antipathy that paranoiac knowledge has for the signifier in the Real, generally more familiar in the schizophrenic. And this, no doubt, is why *Ulysses* so upset Jung who – wishing to become the prophet of a new discourse, becoming indeed the little god of a sect – could only be enraged upon seeing the damage done to the quilting points of a discourse. Fundamentally, Joyce had gone beyond 'the impossibility of a pulverulent discourse' (Aé, p. 379). He had made himself the artisan of a language not consigned to any dictionary, which borrows from them all and says nothing that can be attributed. Thus Joyce – creator of a *neo-world* without recourse to the imagination, for this *neo-world* is mixed with fragments of a world that is not 'neo', in its figures, its words, its images, its places – passed beyond poetry itself, to a place where there is nothing to read, since there is no longer the *One-saying* of the enunciation. Attaining writing without speech, where only the handling of the letter-object remains, Joyce positions himself as the artisan of a proliferating '*motérialité*' which he delivers, like a bone to chew on, to the lucubrations of the commentators. Perhaps I should say he suggests this since, in *Finnegans Wake*, the enigma of the enunciation allows the song to subsist. Joyce becomes like the tenor who sustains the music of the *lalangues*, so much so that this strange text still occasions organised readings. I have attended one or two, and verified the listeners' enchantment. Yet when I asked, they nevertheless confessed to grasping nothing of the text. Quite the posthumous triumph!

Now, the letter without meaning: this is the very paradox of the symptom as Lacan defined it starting from *R.S.I.*, 'an opaque jouissance that excludes meaning' (J/L, p. 36). But here it is not a body symptom. It sets the body aside. This is why, while it interests many people, it does not resonate with anyone's unconscious. This is a writing without flesh, other than that of the verbal elements; and its special capacity to diffract meaning allows for the supposition that this exceptional talent – one could even say this freedom – is, in effect, conditioned by the unknotting of the Imaginary. Between Real and Symbolic, there remains the pure jouissance of multiple letters from multiple languages. Thus, we could say that Joyce does not write with his body. Admittedly, this phrase is not terribly clear. Nevertheless, it must have a basis, given that we commonly speak of those who write 'with their guts'. Surely we can tell that this is not the case for Joyce. Free from the Imaginary, in the Joyce symptom it is the body of the word that is his partner: not the letter of fiction, but the *fixion* of jouissance that excludes both commonplace meaning and the private meaning of the phantasy. It is what makes Joyce 'cancel his subscription to the unconscious' (S, p. 144). If *Finnegans Wake* is read nonetheless, it is because 'one senses the presence of the writer's jouissance' (J/L, p. 25) and this fascinates. As I have said, it is the work of an ungenerous ego and bears the mark of this ego. If we follow Lacan, this is why it does not elicit our sympathy nor touch our unconscious, but only captivates by its strangeness. Was this already the case with the *Epiphanies*?

Return to the epiphanies

'We know the extraordinary destiny of this well-known term over the past few decades of English literary criticism. It serves to designate anything that creates an effect of meaning, of revelation, in a literary work, be it about a character or in regard to plot'. So says Jacques Aubert, in his introduction to the first *Pléiade* volume devoted to Joyce (Joyce and Aubert, 1982, p. LIII). And this is how Joyce, through Stephen, has defined the word:

> By an epiphany, he meant a sudden spiritual manifestation, whether in the vulgarity of speech or of gesture or in a memorable phrase of the mind itself. He believed that it was for the man of letters to record these epiphanies with extreme care, seeing that they themselves are the most delicate and evanescent of moments [. . .] the soul of the commonest object, the structure of which is so adjusted, seems to us radiant.
>
> (SH, p. 213)

Is this a Neo-Platonic legacy via St Thomas? The soul of objects, that is to say, the splendour of being, manifesting itself? But Jacques Aubert makes the point that what Joyce sees there is the action of a spiritual eye, in Joyce's words, the 'gropings of a spiritual eye', (ibid.) even the intimate caresses of a spiritual eye. This displaces the question to the side of the subject, all the more as, according to Aubert, 'an attentive ear will be able to hear, thanks to the homophony eye/I, a spiritual "I", indeed a fantasmatic "I"' (Joyce and Aubert, 1982, p. LIV). In Lacanian terms, this is about the problem of perception, the relation between *percipiens* and *perceptum*, as one used to call 'the long metaphysical coction of science in the School (with the capital *S* our reverence owes it)' (É, p. 531). It is on this point, in his text '*On a Question Prior to Any Possible Treatment of Psychosis*', that Lacan begins to account for the phenomena of hallucinated voices in psychosis. In contrast to all prior theories of perception, the thesis is that the subject is immanent to his perceptions, far from being a mere receiver (see Soler, 2003b). As for what concerns us, if the subject is indeed imminent to his perception, as Lacan was developing at the time, then the question no longer arises of knowing whether the epiphanic manifestation belongs to the thing or to the subject; and Jacques Aubert rightly underscores the ambiguity of the epiphanic phenomenon. But for readers of Lacan, a thesis about the epiphanies was already available.

All epiphanies are fragments of things perceived; as such, they would be homologous to the elementary phenomena of mental automatism, specifically verbal hallucination, once again pointing us towards a hypothesis of psychosis. I myself developed this, but I have revised my view, following a closer reading both of Joyce and of Lacan's re-workings of the concept of the unconscious at the end of his teaching. For sure, one could say that the epiphanies have the same structure as the signifier in the Real: the erratic signifier outside the chain, just like Lacan's definition of the hallucinated mental signifier in '*Question Prior*'. However, they do not have the same subjective function as in psychosis, and this changes everything.

Indeed, I would distinguish between the text of the epiphanies and Joyce's aesthetic theory about them, elaborated in Stephen's voice. I shall begin with the first of these. We know that the stories Joyce grouped together under the title *Epiphanies* are not all of the same kind. They are all small fragments, but some are snippets of things heard, while others are descriptions, almost writing exercises, about various scenes, things observed, personal recollections, evoked in a language that would have justified calling them prose poems as, I believe, Stanislaus Joyce had wished.

As fragments, they are by definition extracts, taken out of context, cut away from their triviality – Joyce's expression – the triviality of the everyday, and therefore outside the obviousness attached to the latter. Many commentators have emphasised the effect of enigma on the reader, to the point of risking a comparison with mystical experience. But let us read, for example, number XX from the *Epiphanies*, written upon the death of Joyce's younger brother, or number XXVII (both published in Scholes and Kain, 1965).

> XX. They are all asleep. I will go up now . . . He lies on my bed where I lay last night! they have covered him with a sheet and closed his eyes with pennies . . . Poor little fellow! We have often laughed together. He bore his body very lightly . . . I am very sorry he died. I cannot pray for him as the others do. Poor little fellow! Everything else is so uncertain!
> (p. 30)

> XXVIII. A moonless night under which the waves gleam feebly. The ship is entering a harbour where there are some lights. The sea is uneasy, charged with dull anger like the eyes of an animal which is about to spring, the prey of its own pitiless hunger. The land is flat and thinly wooded. Many people are gathered on the shore to see what ship it is that is entering their harbour.
>
> (p. 38)

Where is the enigma here? Where is the discordance? There are others like these, highly successful descriptions, poems really, moments taken from everyday life, isolated from their context, especially XXVIII. This focusing, is it not what the camera does when it zooms in on a detail or zooms out to capture a specific scene? And wouldn't this scene easily lend itself to the camera's realism? I could imagine a long shot by Alain Resnais. Or we could take them as exercises in style. So many other similar little texts emerge haphazardly, as if Joyce is somehow getting a feel for writing. Who is to say how the text comes or should come to the writer?

It seems to me that the preoccupation with diagnosis has produced an incomplete and hence biased reading not applicable to all of the *Epiphanies*. Joyce gave a general definition for the epiphany, but they are not all the same.

Some epiphanies demand our attention more than others. Unlike the two cited above, these have nothing to do with sensory or visual memory, but rather with something heard. Hence, they are of the same stuff as hallucinated voices. In them, Joyce carried out veritable removals which clearly rupture the signifying continuity. It is a technique of fragmenting discourse, retaining from it only unstable elements and thereby eroding the obviousness of signification. The *Villanelle of the Temptress* is most often cited here. As noted by Stephen, it was the one that gave him the idea to collect his epiphanies as illustrations of his current aesthetic theory. It belongs to the moment when the young Stephen had already decided that nothing would keep him from his vocational path as a 'man of letters' (SH, 211):

> A young lady was standing on the steps of one of those brown brick houses which seem the very incarnation of Irish paralysis. A young gentleman was leaning on the rusty railings of the area. Stephen as he passed on his quest heard the following fragment of colloquy out of which he received an impression keen enough to afflict his sensitiveness very severely.
>
> *The Young Lady – (drawling discreetly)* . . . O, yes . . . I was . . . at the . . . cha . . . pel . . .

> *The Young Gentleman – (inaudibly) . . . I . . . (again inaudibly) . . . I . . .*
>
> *The Young Lady – (softly) . . . O . . . but you're . . . ve . . . ry . . . wick . . . ed . . .*

In the ellipses, we can discern – as did Jacques Aubert – the hearing of what is not said in what is said, in accordance with the great law of language that is binding for all of us; the epiphany's very title does not fail to direct us to the theme of . . . woman. But we can also say that the epiphanies have the structure of the signifier in the Real, the same structure as that of mental hallucination. I believe it was Catherine Millot who first pointed this out, given that an hallucination is a segment of 'a broken chain' (É, p. 449). Same structure, then, except that Joyce wrote these fragments in a notebook, where they appeared to him worthy of admiration, not aimed at him in the usual way that voices are for the paranoiac; they lack what Lacan called the 'subjective attribution'. This is an important difference. I had the opportunity to hear a patient at Sainte-Anne Hospital who also spoke of 'fragments', fragments heard in passing in the street. But this patient believed they directly concerned him. He added, however, that while he knew the fragments were not really addressed to him, he still could not stop his own thoughts telling him that he was their target. Yet there is nothing of the kind in Joyce.

So then, regarding these epiphanies – with the revelatory value Joyce attributed to them, to which I will return – should we not rather say that they are homologous to the neologising process by which a signifier, whatever it is, acquires for the subject a weight, a scope, a singular value, suddenly stabilising a jouissance that is as ineffable as it is strange, making the enigma of non-meaning pass into certitude? We recognise this process, well-known in psychosis, which goes from enigma to certainty and which was evoked by Lacan in his early writings. But – there is a but – indeed there are several. To begin with, we have Lacan's last elaborations on the function of *lalangue* as constitutive of an unconscious that is not based on meaning, that is, the real unconscious, which implies that all of the unconscious is neologising. Whether in psychosis, neurosis, or perversion, the weight of words, their weight of jouissance – distinct from their meaning – is always singular, unique to the individual. The *motérialité* of the unconscious is thus entirely neologising. This is especially the case for elements that fix the jouissance of the symptom, but not only for these. As Lacan remarked, the interpreting psychoanalyst must attend, as much as possible, to the singular scope of words for his or her analysand.

Indeed, it is interesting to dwell for a moment on the young Stephen's description, exalted but precise, of the process of epiphanisation. An active, wilful process, the effect of 'the gropings of a spiritual eye which seeks to adjust its vision to an exact focus' (SH, p. 211). That focus is beauty, the beauty that the *Nego* refuses to the forms offered him by tradition. To summarise, it is accomplished in three steps: 'First we recognise that the object is *one* integral thing, then we recognise that it is an organised composite structure, a *thing* in fact . . . finally, we recognise that it is *that* thing . . . Its soul, its whatness, leaps to us from the vestment of its appearance' (SH, p. 215). Here we have a resurgence of the Aristotelian imputation of soul to bodies, revisited by St Thomas and the very same idea that Lacan, in *Encore*, puts into question. *Portrait of the Artist* takes a slightly different approach to the redefinition of St Thomas's *Claritas*, proposing, in an equally exalted fashion, epiphanisation not of the Dublin clock but of a basket, that most ordinary of objects. The process similarly results in making *quidditas* surge forth, this time defined as 'the radiance [. . .] the whatness of a thing [. . .] the supreme quality of beauty', which is '[. . .] felt by the artist [. . .] a spiritual state very like to that cardiac condition which the Italian physiologist Luigi Galvani, using a phrase almost as beautiful as Shelley's, called the enchantment of the heart' (PAYM, p. 165). Lacan indicates that he does not much care for this retranslation into aesthetic beauty of the *Claritas* of Being. Granted. But this training of the artist to focus his eye so as to extract the object from its everyday functionality, by a technique of isolation that surrounds it like an invisible circle, elevating its triviality to a new and admirable uniqueness, is this not – metaphysical resonances aside – what Duchamp did with his original *readymades*? A framing function. Besides, do we not perceive here the work of the *Nego* that I evoked, the methodical effort to extract the very perception of things from the *a priori* that conditions and reduces it to the triviality of the shared and the obvious? And then we also know how Joyce, with his full capacity for irony, devalued the memory of this adolescent exaltation: 'Remember your epiphanies on green oval leaves, deeply deep, copies to be sent if you died to all the great libraries of the world, including Alexandria? Someone was to read them there, after a few thousand years [. . .]' (Joyce, 2010, p. 37).

The process is completed by a sort of de-epiphanisation technique, an ironic operation of re-composition, where Joyce amuses himself by confounding the commentators with the reinsertion into his own texts of epiphanic fragments so as to render them unrecognisable. Evidently, this extraction/insertion has to do with the always problematic, always devoid of meaning, place of connection between linguistic units, and also with the fluidity of possible meanings. But since this belongs to literary technique, how can we settle the question of the possibly imposed nature of this phenomenon? At most, we can note Joyce's aptitude for feeling the signifier on its own without its meaning. This aptitude, while not common, is not absent in anyone who speaks. In Joyce, it took on the dimension of a veritable preference for the purely verbal thing and, together with its correlative contempt for meaning, was elevated to the level of a resolute and constant subjective choice. And it is very likely that this aptitude was facilitated by the fault in the Imaginary that Lacan demonstrates, such that the unconscious and the Imaginary were, in atypical fashion, not knotted. It is on this point, at the very end of *The Sinthome*, that Lacan stops: 'It's there for the reading in Joyce that epiphany is what makes it so that, by virtue of the fault, the unconscious and the real are tied together' (S, p. 134).[1]

Hence the ambiguity of these epiphanies, symptoms of the 'slip of the knot', from which Joyce fashioned the material of his literary art. As Lacan noted, we may suspect a phenomenon of imposition here; but, as Lacan also noted, it is no longer recognisable. This is the work of the specific *savoir-faire* (know-how) of the 'premeditated poet', as Joyce designated himself. The same question applies to his art, which seemed to move inexorably toward 'a sort of fracturing, a sort of decomposition', culminating in *Finnegans Wake*, where '. . . there is no longer any phonatory identity' (S, p. 79). Given that Lacan tells us that the words we depend upon are imposed on us, could this be the intrusion of some parasitic wordsmith? Or, by contrast, something welcomed, the poet's search for the phonemic qualities of speech? Put another way, is it Joyce himself who looks for the Real outside the meaning of signifiers, or is it the Real that imposes itself, due to the lack of knotting? Clearly the status of the artist's know-how is at issue here. I will return to this.

In any case, what is sure is that, for Joyce, *lalangue* is manifestly like a thing, a kind of substance for solitary enjoyment. From the *Epiphanies* of the years 1900–1904 – those bits of discourse, taken out of context, subversive of all signification – to the calculated neologisms of *Finnegans Wake*, Joyce produced a paradoxical literature, a literature that separates sense and the letter, that plays with meaning not to sustain or to renew it as does poetry, but to destroy it, leaving only the effect of enigma. Enigma here is uninterpretable as unconscious desire, as Jung was the first to perceive. In a beyond of the witticism which, by contrast, produces an effect of sense from nonsense, Joyce succeeded in opening the field of 'letters' to texts that are excepted from the Symbolic, if indeed the Symbolic is what generates meaning via the linking of signs. This is a strange literature of the Real, owing very little to the Imaginary, and coherent with Joyce's singular ego. It shows us that the Imaginary is not the imagination, something not lacking in Joyce even if, in him, it was quite particular; but that is an altogether different question. Unsubscribed from the unconscious structured like *a* language, Joyce produced a highly particular language of his own that elevates *lalangue*, indeed *lalangues*, to a language made solely of enjoyed signs. This is where his singularity is patent.

So I return to the question: what is it that elevates this writing symptom, between Symbolic and Real, to the status of a Borromean art which, if it is indeed that, must house meaning?

His Enigma-Name

In Joyce, something of meaning remains, even something quite invasive: enigma. The zenith of meaning, if you will. The very tip of an enunciation that does not find its enunciated. Joyce is the 'writer of the enigma par excellence' (S, p. 133) and this is what allows Lacan to say that his art is Borromean without his knowing it, a mark of its authenticity. This, I believe, is the main point of Lacan's interpretation of Joyce. I will return to it in connection with Joyce's know-how. As I have indicated, the *Epiphanies* are not Borromean, for they knot only Symbolic and Real. Nor is the unreadable in *Finnegans Wake*, as it is essentially pure letter which certainly diffracts bubbles of meaning, as I like to call them, but so many that meaning, in the singular, is missing. It is the opposite of free association in analysis where, in wandering from thought to thought, the analysand delineates the unique meaning that is his or her phantasy. No doubt, by privileging the letter, or epiphanic facticity, Joyce enacts his hatred for all commonplace significations. Of course, not just any significations, but those related to his native Ireland, which touched him deeply, in the flesh, we could say, via the mediation of his two 'parents', the double yoke he bore: British Imperialism and the Catholic Church. But, according to Lacan, the enigma is something else; it has another function in Joyce's art. To go straight to the point, it is through enigma that the name is sustained and the ego corrects the slip of the knot. Thus, it is enigma that restores the Borromean function.

I note first that enigma in Joyce is found on two levels. He deliberately stuffed his texts with enigmas, as so many riddles for future Joyceans who, indeed, are very busy trying to solve them. Moreover, he makes use of his epiphanies for this effect. Whether or not something compelled him, he produced enigmas, in the plural. But there is more: *Finnegans Wake*, that dream without waking, which circles round from its last word to its first, is itself a great enigma. There, the fracture of language reaches its peak in equivocation too unbridled to convey a message. As a result, the question of the enunciation – no longer masked by significations of what is said or written – is as much uncovered as it is unresolved. Enigma. For the question is not one of knowing what the statements [*les énoncés*] mean. That is merely false enigma. Each of these statements has its answer, but for every little enigma that is resolved, each time the void of signification is plugged, an altogether different enigma imposes itself: that of the enunciation [*l'énunciation*], the true enigma without answer. Why was such and such utterance produced? Why such and such fragment written here? The book itself is the riddle of all it contains. From Richard Ellmann we know that, as the book neared completion, Joyce amused himself with letting friends guess the name he had chosen for the title of his *work in progress*. Enigma of the enunciation through which Joyce represents himself.

Enunciation, according to Lacan, 'is the enigma raised to the power of writing' (S, p. 133). This thesis applies not only to Joyce but to what is aimed at in psychoanalysis. Not simple, it can be understood only in light of analytic interpretation which, itself, is not always understood.

From Lacan on, analytic discourse has taught us to recognise, paradoxically, 'the written' in the pathways of speech. In psychoanalysis, one does not use a pen, yet something is nevertheless written in the flow of the jouissance of speech, carving out what Lacan calls its 'ravines' (Aé, p. 327) or elsewhere its 'channels' or its 'tracks'. It is carved into the signified, for speech carries more than meaning; it also carries jouissance. Hence, in the speech of an analysand, it is not 'what he says' or what he utters that is to be interpreted. Interpretation aims at the cause of the enunciation as act. It aims at the 'why it is said', and at the 'that it is said', which remains forgotten in what is said (p. 449). It is the cause of the saying – the saying that no word represents – which leaves a trace of writing within the discourse where it is produced. Interpretation aims at this, in clear distinction from hermeneutics. This is why for Lacan the 'I didn't make you say it' (L'é, p. 49) is the minimum interpretation.

Similarly, *Finnegans Wake* – that dream whose dreamer is not one of the characters, but the very dream itself (S, p. 148) – writes nothing other than a saying as 'enigma raised to the power of writing', an enunciation certainly, but one that is undecipherable, whose explanation will not reduce the mystery. As Lacan says, it took Joyce's *savoir-faire* to give *lalangue* a different usage, different from a usage that carries consistent effects of meaning. The methodical foreclosure of anchoring significations leaves only the enigmatic use of pure *signifierness*, the *motérialité* of *lalangue*. Thus, the one who, in *Stephen Hero*, is 'egoistically determined that nothing [. . .] should hinder him from working out the enigma of his position in his own way' (SH, p. 209) manages in the end to be represented by the calculated enigma that is *Finnegans Wake*. Indeed, many of Joyce's traits indicate that he was an enigma to himself, most notably his surprise at being unable to identify with his fellows, an inability to recognise himself in them, always having 'considered himself a being apart, in any order whatsoever' (PAYM, p. 124). But with *Finnegans Wake* – the book with which he most identified, the book with which, in the end, he wanted to construct his stepladder – he has given up solving this enigma. Instead, he lets himself be represented by it, and in a way identifies with it. He uses it as his signature, this name that I will henceforth call his *Name-of-enigma* (*Nom d'énigme*), a name that, as Lacan has shown, sustains the *ego* that corrects the unknotting. Enigma: through it, his art is Borromean; thanks to it, the letters outside meaning – from which both his *Epiphanies* and *Finnegans Wake* are made – link up the Imaginary to this pinnacle of meaning that is the enigma.

I note as well, in *Portrait of the Artist*, the connection between proper name and enigmatic being that we find so clearly in the episode about Stephen's journey to Cork with his father. Following what he describes as a strange, disquieting moment of derealisation which leaves him without any boundaries, he clings on to proper and common names, which he even writes backwards, in an order about which there would be much to say.

> . . . he repeated slowly to himself: – I am Stephen Daedalus. I am walking beside my father whose name is Simon Daedalus. We are in Cork, in Ireland. Cork is a city. Our room is in the Victoria Hotel. Victoria and Stephen and Simon. Simon and Stephen and Victoria. Names.
>
> (*PAYM*, p. 70)

Indeed, what is proper to the name is that it is admitted in the Other, just like the signifier. But the difference is that the name does not predicate, it does not say anything about the being of the one named. For this reason, it can constitute an anchoring point when the sense of identity vacillates. I will return to this.

Nevertheless, Lacan asked about 'where significance *qua* written starts to be distinct from mere effects of phonation. Phonation is what transmits the proper function of the name' (S, p. 61). I pause here, because this statement, depending on how one reads it, might appear to be an objection to what I have just said about the writing of an enigmatic name.

If phonation denotes the sonic register of the heard (as opposed to the graphic register of the seen) and therefore denotes the *sensorium* that supports the signifier, would Lacan's phrase not mean that the song's melody matters more than its signifyingness? The music captured by the ear is certainly what makes *l'homme/LOM*, or *je nomme/jeune homme* sound the same. Thus we need the orthographic written to reveal the equivocation of the sound unit. This is why Lacan said that the only lapsus is the lapsus of the pen. But phonation does not belong to the register of equivocation between the heard and the written. Would phonation then be the voice? Not according to Lacan. Every signifying chain imposes itself in its dimension of voice and does so for everyone who speaks. Regarding the hallucinated voice, Lacan notes in 'Question prior' that 'it is a mistake to take verbal hallucinations to be auditory in nature, when it is theoretically conceivable that it not be auditory at all [. . .] for example [. . .] some non-auditory register of hallucinatory spelling out of words' (É, p. 446). What constitutes the hallucinated voice is not any specific sensory medium. Just as the gaze is an object, and is not reducible to the eye, so the voice is distinct from the auditory and is not necessarily vocal. It was with remarks about the voice that Lacan began his lecture entitled *La Troisième*, delivered in Rome in 1974. It was an opportunity for him 'to empty it of any substance there could be in the noise that it makes, that is, to return it back to the signifying operation, the one I have specified as the speech effects of metonymy' (Lacan, 1975c, p. 177). The voice is an object, a way of saying that it would not be an exaggeration to speak of the voiceless voice. Is it not in fact through the written letter that Joyce has given voice? This in no way contradicts Lacan's insistence on saying that, in the written letter, it is not the meaning that matters but the music and rhythm, as it leaves quite specifically a place for the enigma of the enunciation.

Phonation is neither the equivocation proper to *lalangue* nor is it the object voice. Phonation is the production of the text, the emission that causes it to be perceived in one form or another. It is the signifier's act of emission, without which there would be no name whatsoever. With interpretation, we must therefore distinguish its phonation – its '*jaculation*', says Lacan – from what it states, its text. It is an open question in analysis to know which of these is more operative. In analysis, phonation is necessarily oral, but could it not also be graphic, the *jaculation-phonation* of what is scrawled on paper in, for example, 'Inspired writings'? Understood as '*jaculation*', phonation is enunciation's existential position; and in Joyce, it is the unique saying of the enigma. It was through this that the unique aim of his art was realised and a sinthome was created, achieving a plugging – with his Enigma-Name – of the void with which he had equated his father.

Note

1 See the knot on p. 72 where the I is unknotted while the R and the S are tied together.

Chapter 7

The Stepladder

We still need to examine the value of this supplementation. It is a substitution sinthome, but does this imitation work as well as the father version of the sinthome? What Lacan could say, without specifying it further, was that he had revived this ancient spelling on account of the two slopes of Joyce's work. Two slopes: what are they? One is, no doubt, that he enjoyed the letter, between Symbolic and Real, which says nothing and is unreadable. The other is the saying of the enigma which, beyond any proclamation, positions the artist and renames the one who refused to be named on the basis of a genealogical tree. Side by side in Joyce, there are certainly works in which his own truth is at stake – works such as *Stephen Hero*, *Portrait of the Artist*, even *Exiles*, where he seeks his own being, seeks to decipher the riddle of himself – and works in which we perceive the symptomatic, opaque jouissance of the real letter, which does not ask for anything from anyone. It is, nevertheless, a tour de force, for with this calculated unreadability, Joyce succeeded in advancing the Borromean function of his Enigma-Name, such that Lacan could say of *Finnegans Wake* that Joyce had given it '... the function of being his stepladder' (J/L, p. 26).

The stepladder was introduced by Lacan in his first lecture on Joyce. That little household item which allows one access to the book on the highest shelf or, for that matter, to the jar of preserves, lends itself as a metaphor for all the instruments of self-promotion, all the stepping stones of ambition. We refer to people who 'elevate themselves to greatness', 'climb the social ladder'. Sometimes, pompously, we even call it sublimation. Thus, with a chortle, Lacan says: '*Hissecroitbeau, LOM*' (ibid., p. 31). Thanks to the French language, beauty – so essential to Joyce – has its place of honour in the middle of the phrase. But in the end, Joyce found himself not through beauty – we hardly speak of beauty in regard to *Finnegans Wake* – but through enigma, as I have said before. Was beauty his stepladder?

Certainly not. With the dream that is *Finnegans Wake*, the dream of a treatise on aesthetics, *Claritas* and *quiddity* – the young Stephen's dream – is well and truly forgotten. What then about posturing? Is this his stepladder? Indeed. Joyce, with his minimal theatricality, shows himself in his uniqueness. This is a narcissism altogether different from that of the mirror stage, which is based on an image and given to the child '. . . as the contour of his stature . . .' Joyce's narcissism, however, lacks a mirror, and involves an elusive exceptionalism, unless one considers the reading public – which elevated him into posterity – to be some sort of mirror.

But here there is a question: what did he obtain from this? Lacan asks: what point did Joyce reach?

A not so proper name

To the singular ego that Lacan diagnosed, the ego that makes him what he says he is, namely 'a being apart', we must add: a name that is no less singular, 'something strange in Joyce [. . .] what Joyce valorises at the expense of the father' (S, p. 73). But Lacan makes it more precise: in Joyce, 'the proper name does all it can to make itself more than the S1, the master signifier. . .' (ibid.). Proper name, master signifier. They are different. The latter represents the subject, but for other signifiers, S2, which endeavour to predicate what this represented *is*. In contrast, the Name, when it is indeed proper, excludes predicates, ascribes no qualities to the one named, says nothing really about its *quiddity*, nor about its 'soul' or its 'essence'. The proper name is not epiphanic; it is only an index, what Kripke called a 'rigid designator'. Certainly there is great debate on this point. Russell, for example, postulates that a proper name could include some property, specifically when this property is itself unique, such as 'author of Waverley', which constitutes a proper name just as much as the patronymic 'Walter Scott' since, for this work, there is only one author. Frege dethroned this concept, as Lacan mentions in Seminar XVIII, *D'un discours qui ne serait pas du semblant*, but here I note something else. When a proper name is constituted by a property, the proper name moves closer to the master signifier and the '*I am*' of the one named goes toward the predicate, toward an S2: '*I am . . . the author of Waverley*'. This S2, in turn, can relate to other signifiers: 'the author of Waverley' is . . . whatever one likes. Thus, when the signifier constitutes the name, the name drifts towards the surname – James Joyce named Dedalus – and even toward the common noun.

But 'Joyce [. . .] wanted to have nothing other than the stepladder of magisterial saying' (J/L, p. 33). And, indeed, through magisterial saying, he made his name known. Lacan's formulation points to a subjective choice, the choice of not passing either by way of the body or by way of the 'stepladder of castration' that characterises the saint. The very spelling of *sinthome*, via homophony, evokes the question of knowing whether or not this son of the Jesuits would be a saint, a term that Lacan applied to the psychoanalyst. Lacan's answer is unequivocal. 'Joyce is not a saint. He *enjoys* too much the S.K. Beau, from his art, he takes an art-pride that is unquenchable' (ibid.). Let us say that he makes himself beautiful, or even that he plays at being the beautiful and promotes himself by his magisterial saying. In fact, it was not only a name that he wanted, but a referent name, a name that would defy all predicates while also eliciting them. What could be better than the Enigma-Name *we* discussed above: 'I' am . . . what my dream represents, the enigma of *Finnegans Wake*. And Joyceans took up the challenge, producing a whole constellation of predicates supposed to resolve the enigma. Why not *Joyce the dédale(us), Joyce the unreadable, Joyce the languages*, even *Joyce the enigma*, etc., until we come to *Joyce the symptom* which is something completely different. I will come back to this.

Nevertheless, with respect to Joyce's magisterial saying, Lacan tells us that 'after so much attention to shovelling in publicity, in the end what he got, because of the way he got it, was not worth much' (ibid.). A strange evaluation, parallel to the one about his wife: of no use to him. It invites us to question the scope of the Joycean supplementation and, let us say, its benefits since, regarding his wish to have a name that would last forever, he already had this.

What went wrong with the original knot for Lacan to say that what Joyce obtained from it was not worth much? What had he missed other than not obtaining it in the more ordinary way via the father version of the sinthome?

If we take his life as testimony, we cannot ignore that this 'necessary son' – if he saved himself from paternal emptiness, if he made himself an exception – saves himself alone. Far from being a saviour, he included neither his children nor even his chosen Nora in his salvation. This is due to the social link he established, a link that, like him, is very particular. By designating 'the only arms I allow myself to use – silence, exile, and cunning' (PAYM, p. 191). Joyce himself allows us to recognise its limits. A social link, as Lacan defines it, establishes, by way of language – more than a simple proximity among beings – a solidarity of bodies and, most notably, a knotting of the generations and of the sexes. But a mass of readers more or less identified with each other and linked to the *Enigma-Name* promoted by the book of enigmas is in itself something else; and we might also ask if the number of letters Joyce wrote, signed, and addressed did not have the function, among others, of compensating for the a-corporality of this link and of his name. 'Since man's got a body, it is by the body that he can be got', and therefore 'deportees alone take part in history' (J/L, p. 34). Nothing of the kind for Joyce, in spite of his exile which confirmed the seriousness of his judgement about history: nothing happens. We learn about this from his writings, from the famous 'book of himself' for, personally, he knows nothing of solidarity. The sole thing that matters to him is style. With the First World War in full swing, this is what he tells Stanislaus who endeavours to interest him in the events of that terrible time. Flat refusal on the part of Joyce.

Nor did Joyce, writer that he was, save literature. Lacan's verdict is well-known: he left it in ruins, dealt the fatal blow, although its death throes have gone on for a long time. In Lacan's reading, it is a case of the letter killing literature. And literary criticism? Is that also finished? Of course, not all of it is of value, but all literary dreams are written 'for the governing of the body, for the *corpo-rections*, regarding which (Joyce) has the last word, known as *daysens*, the literary symptom's meaning brought into the light of day, available at last for consumption' (J/L, p. 36). What can we say except that meaning always has to do with the body? Indeed, this is where the symbolic is incorporated. And is it not true that 'good sense' and the correction, *corpo-rection*, administered to a child go hand in hand? This is because, in the metonymy of speech, what is displaced is the jouissance that words convoke, the jouissance that *lalangue* civilises, beyond the lack of the object that haunts their interval. It is *lalangue* that gives jouissance its mature form, standardised around the holes of the body that it eroticises. Henceforth, there is an equivalence between what comes out of those holes, be it excrement or the voice of the signifier. It is *joui-sense*. Hence Lacan's falsely irreverent remark about the 'roll of toilet paper from which letters are pulled off' (ibid.). He was speaking about letters belonging to '*literature*', not those of Joyce, which are outside literature. Joyce himself says it: letter, litter, the letter as waste, *Sicut palea.* Right there we have St Thomas. There is, however, the opaque jouissance of the non-literary symptom, a different jouissance and, according to Lacan, the only one that wakes us from the dream of meaning.

The dream of the awakened

With the question of awakening, where did Joyce finally end up, he who had mocked 'a certain Doctor Jung (the Swiss Tweedledum not to be confused with the Viennese Tweedledee, Dr. Freud' for amusing himself '. . . at the expense (in every sense of the word) of ladies and gentlemen who are troubled with bees in their bonnets' (SL, p. 282)? Was it in the name of his own awakening that he engaged in this ridicule and imputation of greed?

When Freud, speaking of his nocturnal dreams, recognised the royal road to the unconscious, it was because he added to the simple narrative of the dream its associations, which made deciphering possible, and from this deciphering, a delivery of meaning. His technique goes well beyond the enigmatic emergence of dreams, always fascinating to humanity, to the meaning one hopes will illuminate it. But Freud also says that the dream itself is at the service of the desire to sleep; it is a fiction that softens the demands of the drives by channelling them into the networks of its scenario. Thus we understand the nightmare which wakes us as a failure.

> Just as we speak about screen memories, we can say that the dream is a screen-dream. It is not so much that it lies. Rather it keeps brute jouissance at a distance, tames the life of the body into the homeostases and derivatives of the pleasure principle, which has no other meaning than the damping down of jouissance. Dreaming is therefore a defence, a particular case of defence against the Real. Whence the paradox: the royal road misses what analysis is aiming at, that we link the Real, the jouissance which sows discord in the symptom, the symptom which is not a dream.
>
> (Soler, 1999)

When I say that psychoanalysis aims at the Real, or rather a Real, this is, of course, according to Lacan.

So we wake up from a nightmare in order to go on sleeping, to sleep the waking dream of adjustment to a reality where the Symbolic and Imaginary govern and the pleasure principle is king. Paradoxically we see that the insomniac is the most incorrigible of sleepers, the one who finds shelter from nightmares! Indeed, relative to the Real that is outside meaning for the one who speaks, the Symbolic and Imaginary engender nothing but the dream. With these, we can tell stories, some beautiful, others less so, but always stories and, in the best of cases, myths, such as Oedipus. About reality itself, we will certainly not say with Calderón that it is a dream, but rather that it comes already woven with the linguistic, Symbolic relations that order it. Whence the suspicion we sometimes have that everything is but phantasy and that the Real escapes those who enter the network of discourse. Consequently, ordinary people – enveloped in the dream that is discourse, dwelling in the social link with its cocoon of prejudices – sometimes aspire to waking. This is a crucial question for psychoanalysis, which is a discourse, a social link, with no instrument other than language.

This theme insists in Lacan, regarding 'the jouissance proper to the symptom'. In the end, he defines it as 'the opaque jouissance that excludes meaning' (J/L, p. 36). As he noted and I have said: 'There is no waking except through this jouissance', jouissance untied from the knots of the Imaginary and Symbolic. Thus great importance is attached to awakening, but what value does it have for psychoanalysis and for Joyce?

In *Joyce le symptôme II*, Lacan answers unambiguously: psychoanalysis devalues opaque jouissance, the only jouissance that awakens, depreciates it by 'resorting to meaning in order to resolve it . . .' There is 'no awakening except by this jouissance [. . .] no chance to arrive there except by being the dupe . . . of the father, as I have pointed out' (ibid.). Dupe of the father, this means dupe of the *sinthome* that makes a knot between meaning and the Real. This, Lacan explains, is an analytic operation. To obtain meaning, we perform a splice between Imaginary and Symbolic (unconscious knowledge) and 'with the same stroke we make another one, precisely between that which is symbolic and the real [. . .] between [the] *sinthome* and the parasitic real of jouissance' (S, p. 58). Put another way, we make this jouissance enter into the Borromean knot.

What does it mean for Joyce that his writing – outside meaning, save for the enigma, as I noted above – seems to be identified with waking? Without exaggeration, we could even say that everything we know about his stance constituted him as one awakened from the sleep of reality, for example, the distance he took from the family dream, from his city, from his native Ireland which, according to his brother Stanislaus, was responsible for giving him his oft-referred to superlative vitality. There is also his lucidity and his ability to withstand ordeals, the even temper that earned him the nickname 'Sunny James'. In brief, a sort of impenetrability that a psychiatrist would certainly consider pathological, yet definitely gives him the profile of someone who has been awakened. This is how Lacan speaks of him in the very same passage where he emphasises the opaque jouissance of his symptom. The passage is widely quoted, but without further delving into it. How should we take this paragraph about Joyce, who was so awake as to be offensive, with a wish to wake up literature by ending it and suffocating the dream? Just after Lacan states that psychoanalysis depreciates this opaque jouissance, he says: 'What is extraordinary is not that Joyce arrived there without Freud [. . .] but without recourse to the experience of analysis' (J/L, p. 36). Arrived at what? The syntax of the phrase leaves no doubt: he arrived at the same devaluation of an opaque jouissance by meaning as does psychoanalysis when it makes itself the dupe of the Father. This is Lacan's thesis, that Joyce the sinthome performed an operation homologous to the analytic operation of depreciating opaque jouissance through meaning.

Where can we discern this operation? No doubt in the fact that Joyce, far from contenting himself with the jouissance of the letter, which does not ask anything from anyone, wished to publish, as Lacan noted. Joyce passionately wanted a name, even before making a name for himself. But there is no name except within the social link. This was clearly more important to him than the opaque jouissance of *lalangue*. The one awakened from autistic jouissance outside meaning and outside a social link thus aspired to a dream that corrects, to a link, and to a substitutive Imaginary. We can sense this insofar as, whenever Joyce evokes Stephen's difference, his foreignness and separateness from his comrades, he is astonished by it. We can also sense it in the nostalgia that is regularly added to his ironic and critical observation; and in his satisfaction each time he notes the least stirring of affect. Besides, is *Finnegans Wake* not a dream? We see the paradox: the dream is made for sleep, *dixit* Freud, but this dream, fully saturated with the jouissance that wakes, does not awake; indeed, it does not end, finishing with the article '*the*' that was missing from its first phrase, '*riverrun*'. Joyce claims to have written it the way one thinks in dreams, in the nocturnal realm of sleep where, he adds, humanity spends a third of its life. Paradoxically, as well, it is a dream he shares, aspiring to capture the reader in a work sufficiently proliferating and circular as to last forever, thus making himself last forever, or at the very least 'for centuries'. A nightmare, says Lacan, but one from which there is no more waking. For Joyce – using his enigma as bait – had tossed a bone to his readers, ever voracious for mulling over riddles. A bone to chew on: an *osbjet*. At the cost of this splicing, something is accomplished, an operation that, thanks to the *ego of enigma*, successfully knots the letter's opaque jouissance to the continuous creation of readers. We might also attach a bit more importance to the title Joyce chose, to the fact that, in English, *wake* refers, not only to waking, but also to a vigil, usually a vigil for the dead. The title actually originates in a popular Irish song which tells of one Tom Finnegan who came back to life during his funeral wake. Would it then be too much to say that the *wake* of *Finnegans Wake* evokes, indeed summons, a paradoxical resurrection of the social link? Didn't Joyce wish to be the inventor of a 'participatory' oeuvre that could not work without the contribution of its readers? After all, in response to a question by Max Eastman, quoted by Ellmann, he said: 'The demand that I make of my reader is that he should devote his whole life to reading my work' (Ellmann, 1982, p. 703). His whole life, nothing less. He further described his 'ideal reader' as someone 'suffering from ideal insomnia' (ibid.). To put it another way, I would say that, if dreamers of reality can dream of waking up from the Real of opaque jouissance, the one wakened from the Real outside meaning dreams the opposite: a dream that never ends and is shared.

The extraordinary thing is not so much that Joyce dreamt of his name as the principle of a secular social link, but that he made it happen, made his proper name, his ego, the referent of the little world of Joyceans, and even succeeded (with the help of Jacques Lacan and Jacques Aubert) in sparking the interest of a number of psychoanalysts. This path is the very opposite to that of the ordinary analysand who, at best, manages to utilise a bit of the Real outside meaning to put an end to his transference dream. Joyce, on the other hand, went from the Real of his symptoms – his *Nego* to the Other, his taste for *lalangue*, his distance from his fellows – to what I will venture to call the artist's novel. But is it even possible to speak of a novel when corrosive equivocations abolish narrative itself? A novel, nonetheless, one that is read even though it says nothing, save for the enigma of a written enunciation. Without that, we might have seen in Joyce an extreme *narcynicism*, condensing narcissism and cynicism, the posture of a subject fully occupied with the construction of his own stepladder, but also having no other purpose than his own jouissance. When all is said and done, this was not the case for Joyce.

Thus, whether we say *symptom*, *sinthome*, even *joui-sens*, we always have proof by Joyce: supreme jouissance of the *letter-fixion*, the *saying-sinthome* that renames, enigma as the substitute for all *sens-joui*, altogether different from both *common joui-sens* and the *joui-sens* of the phantasy. This is why, after designating Joyce a Father of deo-logue, Lacan makes him the representative of – symptomatology. As for the symptom, Joyce shows its 'apparatus, essence, abstraction' (J/L, p. 25). For without knowing it, he maintained it at the level of its 'logical consistency' (p. 35). We must hear this phrase in its full weight, coming as it does from Lacan's pen. In *La Logique du Fantasme*, he had already distinguished two types of consistency for the *objet a*: logical consistency and bodily consistency. Its logical consistency denotes its place and function in the topology of the subject, whereas its bodily consistency results from the fact of its incarnation as a piece of the body, a piece detached by the effect of language (breast, excrement, gaze, voice), that lodges in structure as a *plus de jouir* (surplus jouissance), at the very place where the signifier is missing. For the symptom also, there are always two consistencies at stake. In general, the symptom is both a product of language and a 'body event'. But strictly speaking, this is not the case for Joyce, who retains only the symptom's logical consistency, given that his symptomatic jouissance of the letter elevates *lalangue* to language without passing through the Imaginary of the body. He also illustrates the *sinthome* function, yet by disallowing its incarnation in the genealogical tree, he retains only the logical, Borromean function of knotting without a father. With his highly atypical triple series – the symptomatic *fixion* of real jouissance, the *sinthomatic nomination* that ex-ists and knots, the enigma that reintroduces the *dit-mention* of meaning – he will have made 'a tour of the reserve' (J/L, p. 189) of the unconscious, of everything one could use to construct a stepladder. But from each he will have retained only the abstraction, the logic.

Chapter 8
Art-dirp

As I have said, the symptom name that Lacan gave Joyce was not among the various names – moving towards common nouns – that Joyce might ever have anticipated. It is true that the difference is not readily visible at the level of the form of the name. Nevertheless, the symptom name does *more* than a master signifier, insofar as it does not elicit predicates in the way a master signifier does; and specifically, it is made from something else: it is a product of the *savoir-faire* of the working artist. Indeed, this name is made from his art – Borromean, as I have said – doubtless without his knowing it and different from such names as hero or artist, formulated from his magisterial saying. Lacan often insists on this dimension, an effect produced by the working artist's know-how. Here the effect is correction of the slip of the knot. Certainly 'wanting a name', something obvious in Joyce but hardly his only characteristic, would not have been enough. We can say the same thing about his sound logic: he conforms to it, but it is 'made solely from his art' and without his perceiving it.

The nomination prompts the following question: 'How can an art target in an expressly divinatory way the substantialisation of the *sinthome* in its consistence, but also in its existence and in its hole?' (S, p. 28). It is a way of asking how Joyce could sustain a Borromean knot since, according to Lacan, consistency, existence, and hole are respectively the attributes of the Imaginary, Real, and Symbolic. Indeed, I see here the main question of the seminar, for it implies that '*art-dire*' rivals the father function and, regarding the father, permits Joyce 'to bypass him' (p. 110). We clearly sense that what is at stake in this thesis is not limited to Joyce but involves everything Lacan promoted in terms of the 'beyond of the Oedipus', specifically psychoanalysis which, if we are to believe him, 'when it succeeds, proves that the Name-of-the-Father can just as well be bypassed' (p. 116).

Joyce's praxis

According to Lacan, the re-knotting in Joyce is the product of *savoir-faire*; and *savoir-faire*, by definition is that which has no guarantor for its knowledge. Yet the essential point here is that one 'is only responsible within the limits of his savoir-faire' (S, p. 47). Lacan, in fact, holds Joyce responsible for his blindly acquired *supplementation* to the point of crediting him with it, even though he knew nothing of what he was doing. 'Joyce did not know that he was fashioning the sinthome, I mean, that he was simulating it. He was oblivious to it and it is by dint of this fact that he is a pure artificer, a man of *savoir-faire*, which is what is likewise known as artist' (p. 99). Lacan often said, about artists in general, but specifically about the surrealists: 'they really didn't know what they were doing' (NDP, 9 April 1973/74). The same for poets. Like them, Joyce was justified in deriving from his art his 'pride [*art-gueil*] to the point of satiation' (J/L, p. 33). Lacan even seems to think that Joyce would have accepted the name he gives him, the name of his *savoir-faire*: the symptom. But this is merely a supposition for, without him, how could we know?

Savoir-faire, says Lacan, 'endues a remarkable quality to the art of which one is capable, because there is no Other of the Other to perform the Last Judgment' (S, p. 47).

In *Les non-dupes errent*, he was already speaking of 'a primordial value'. But with no Other of the Other, this remarkable value is nothing other than a value remarked by others. And like a 'leg up', the stepladder of art cannot be constructed all alone; there must be others. These others, from the moment one addresses them with a request, become Others with a capital O. Lacan says: 'The Other of the real Other, that is, the impossible, is the idea that we form of artifice, inasmuch as it is a form of making which eludes our grasp, that is, which far exceeds the jouissance we can derive from it' (S, p. 50). And also: 'This means there is something from which we cannot derive jouissance' (p. 47).

Here, then, is the difference between know-how (*savoir-faire*) and knowledge (*savoir*). This statement has its foundation in *Encore*, where we learn that unconscious knowledge, made from *lalangue*, is enjoyed in the symptom; and that speaking is (also) a jouissance. But *savoir-faire* is different. In *The Sinthome*, Lacan says it is necessary instead to posit that the artifices of *savoir-faire*, remarkable because they are remarked, are not enjoyed: or at least, they go beyond the jouissance that we could get from them. Who is this 'we' that does not derive enjoyment from them? Is it those who give a 'leg up' to the artificer, Joyce's public, his readers? Or is it the artificer himself? It is difficult to think that it is the artificer, given how much of the author's jouissance is perceived in the work that is his stepladder.

The artificer's art has the same value as the Other of the real Other; in other words, it is something he alone enjoys, something that – Lacan insists – remains 'off limits' to the reader. Hence the question I have already broached: why did Joyce publish? Indeed, his verbal games, even if fascinating, are also tiring. They do not touch our unconscious; they are not consonant with it. According to Lacan, Joyce is so 'unsubscribed' from the unconscious that his 'private jokes' leave us untouched. Thus, as illustrated in Joyce, there is something in the *savoir-faire* that we cannot enjoy. And Lacan adds: 'Let us call it God's jouissance' (S, p. 47). Surprising, is it not? This echoes a remark in '*La méprise du sujet supposé savoir*' where Lacan made Joyce one of the three Fathers of the *deo-logue*, alongside Moses and Meister Eckhart (Aé, p. 337). In reality, this is more than an echo; it is a step. For if art constitutes the Other of the real Other, this is never without jouissance and therefore amounts to more than *deo-logue*. Logic, including the logic of dialogues, is foreign to jouissance and, according to Lacan, always at risk for 'turning skepticism into superstition' (Aé, p. 427). In Joyce, Lacan recognised what he calls 'sound logic', but even more than that, the jouissance that alone can render the Other consistent and, without which, the Other, reduced to the subject supposed to knowledge is 'a little unwell' (p. 337). The artist makes something more than dialogue. Thus, a divine artist . . .

God the creator: imputed to have forged the Universe, to have moulded it the same way an artisan potter moulds his pot. Today, the image of the potter has certainly been relegated to the past; those in the know – in this age of science – speak instead of 'intelligent design'. Either way, a successful work upholds the hypothesis of an artificer, the very same that Joyce invokes in the last lines of *A Portrait of the Artist*. 'He is the one who knows, who knows what he has to do' (S, p. 56). And furthermore, Lacan notes that for Joyce, in *Stephen Hero* and *Portrait*, 'the artist is not the redeemer, it is God himself, as an artificer' (S, p. 65). Indeed, for Joyce – if in fact one could doubt God – one does not doubt. Hence the artist acquires a remarkable value equal to that of . . . God.

So then, what is there to say about Joyce's not insignificant *savoir-faire?* Lacan's thesis on this point is not the one usually ascribed to him, for it is eclipsed by what he develops in the very same seminar, about Joyce's writing which, itself, caused a lot of ink to flow. It is a singular writing that becomes more and more so over time, moving toward what Lacan calls a 'sort of fracturing', a 'dissolution of language' culminating in *Finnegans Wake*, so that in the end 'there is no longer any phonatory identity' (S, p. 79).

But, according to Lacan, Joyce's praxis is not his *savoir-faire* with the letter – about which we have no indication that it was something imposed on him – rather, it is 'something that emanates from the *dire*, from the fact of saying, from what on this occasion I shall call *art-dire* [art-saying], to slide towards ardour' (S, p. 99). And we know Joyce was not lacking in ardour. *Art-dire* (art-saying) was necessary to compete with the *dire* (saying) that knots the three registers. Put another way, for the divine artist, his symptom name did far more than the master signifier he had wished for himself. It was a name with no synonyms, a name which could veer neither toward a surname nor toward a common noun, a name of exception. Thus, the power of *savoir-faire* will have made up for, through the *art-dire*, the transmission by a father – since for Lacan, from *L'étourdit* on, the father function is a function of the *saying-sinthome* that conditions the knotting of the three consistencies.

The operation of speech

It is noteworthy that from the beginning of *The Sinthome*, Lacan had at his disposal the thesis of supplementation through art. In the second lesson and again in the third, he asserts it even before demonstrating it: 'Joyce happens, through his art, to have aimed in a privileged way at the fourth term known as the sinthome' (S, p. 27). But one cannot think that this is the object of the seminar. We need to reiterate what it is that renders efficacious the Borromean *art-dire*, if we do not wish to wallow in the religion of art. Joyce arrived there, but not through the workings of the Holy Spirit; and Lacan sought to explain it by way of, among other things, the phallus.

We grasp the logic of this approach by recalling Lacan's first elaborations, well before the schema of the Borromean knot, starting from the paternal metaphor. What these postulate, more than a solidarity between Father function and phallic function, is a clear subordination, echoing the more global subordination between Imaginary and Symbolic that is written into the metaphor and into every schema of this preliminary period,

Schemas L and R. Whence the idea that, in psychosis, the phallic function is missing, along with its sexuating identifications and the jouissances they allow. Schreber provides proof. With the Borromean knot, the Symbolic's stranglehold on the Imaginary is challenged and the question becomes one of the knotting of the three equivalent consistencies: Real, Symbolic, Imaginary. The entire earlier clinic then needs to be rethought on the basis of this knotting by the *sinthome*. This raises the question: what becomes of the phallic function when there is a supplementation to the *Father sinthome*, when the 'outside discourse' has thereby found its solution?

When there is Borromean knotting of the three consistencies, two jouissances are distinguished in it: the jouissance of meaning between Symbolic and Imaginary, and phallic jouissance between Symbolic and Real. We see this written in the plane projection of the knot:

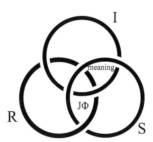

But conversely, when the jouissances are attested to, they produce a test of the knotting. This is what Lacan brings to light in Joyce. Meaning, more precisely *joui-sens*, is jeopardised by the dropping of the body, the unknotting from the Imaginary. But meaning maintained in the form of the enigma, with the Enigma-Name, signals that there is a re-knotting of the Imaginary by the *ego-sinthome*. Similarly, phallic jouissance is sustained by Joyce's writing, without the father, according to Lacan's hypothesis. So once again, we have the question of the re-emergence of what Lacan had called the phallic function. Certainly it implies a jouissance, but one that has fallen under the blow of a castration.

Lacan says: 'One believes oneself to be a male because one has a little scrap of a dick' (S, p. 7). But also: 'It takes more than that'. What more? For many years, and again in *L'étourdit*, Lacan answers: the phallus. Very many analyst readers of Lacan have concluded that, capitalised or not, the phallus does not go without the Father. But Lacan says explicitly: 'The phallus is the conjunction between what I've called *this parasite*, which is the scrap of a dick in question, and the function of speech' (S, ibid.). Indeed, a few months earlier in his *Geneva Lecture*, this is how he had situated the early formation of symptoms, as a conjunction, but more than a conjunction, a 'coalescence' of the *motérialité* of the unconscious derived from spoken *lalangue* with the sexual reality of that little bit of dick. He illustrated it with the case of Little Hans. Taken literally, these developments dismantle the solidarity between the phallic signifier and the father, unless one says there is no speech without the father. I will come back to this!

As for phallic jouissance, to which Lacan returns in this seminar, he says it is 'located at the conjunction between the Symbolic and the Real'. This is the very place, I will note, where he situates Joyce's epiphanies, as well as the writing of *Finnegans Wake*. He further clarifies that phallic jouissance is to be distinguished from that of the penis, which enjoys in the eroticism of the Imaginary of the body and its orifices. As for phallic jouissance, it is 'the locus of that which in consciousness is denoted by the *parlêtre* as might' (S, p. 44). Indeed, there is a power to conjoin speech and a certain so-called phallic jouissance, which 'is experienced, given the fact of the *parlêtre*, as parasitic' (ibid.)

A power, then, that speech has to generate jouissance, the jouissance of speech beyond the body. And to complete what he said about Joyce's art as a supplementation to his phallic position, Lacan adds: 'And this is always the way. The phallus is the conjunction between what I've called this *parasite*, which is the little scrap of dick in question, and the function of speech' (S, p. 7).

I am emphasising this phrase: 'And this is always the way'. It is clearly understood here that the jouissance represented as power is not found solely in the bedroom. It can, of course, invest the organ, but it is everywhere that language is employed, in politics, in literature, etc. For Joyce, his art can restore phallic jouissance using only the linguistic instrument. Perhaps we would not say the same for painting or music, I am not sure, but for whoever speaks or writes, this ciphered jouissance drifts in speech, without convoking the father.

By way of objection to this phallic function without the father but with speech, could we not say that speech, as construed by Lacan, implies the father as signifier, functioning as a quilting point for the whole edifice of language? And did Lacan not demonstrate that, in psychosis, in Schreber's case where the function is missing, the very structure of speech is modified, and that, in the absence of this quilting point, both identity and jouissance are disrupted? This in fact was Lacan's first thesis: subordination of phallic signification to the paternal metaphor, subordination of the Imaginary to the Symbolic. In 1975, having reworked his concept of the unconscious, Lacan also reworked his concept of speech.

It is no longer the intersubjective speech of '*Function and Field*', which institutes the partner, saying 'you are my master', or 'you are my wife'. This full speech was considered to be connected to the paternal function. But, as Lacan realised and remarked in *D'un discours qui ne serait pas du semblant*, full speech is simply speech that fills, and what could it fill except the hole of the missing sexual relation, which is exactly what the father symptom does. There where full speech is, there is nothing but a plug, and a fragile one at that, for the non-relation pushes toward a homophony: '*tué ma femme*' (kill my wife) (see Lacan, 1990a, p. 38). In general in 1975, under Lacan's pen, speech became the *blablabla* of chit-chat, no longer valued as anchoring signification, but rather enjoyed and intrinsically generative of phallic meaning. Also from then on, the relation of speech to the Father required revisions which Lacan himself made. For, in fact, this reversal does not date from the seminar on Joyce.

Over the years, Lacan regularly returned to what he called the *Bedeutung* of the phallus. He says it is the only complete genitive. Indeed, it is simultaneously signifier and signified. On the one hand, the phallus is 'the signifier that is destined to designate meaning effects as a whole, insofar as the signifier conditions them by its presence as signifier' (É, p. 579), thus the signifier that denotes the power of the signifier as such. On the other hand, in every case, the chain of speech signifies the phallus, given the structure of referring, signifier to signifier, signification to signification, that is to say, the impossibility of gathering together the totality of signifiers. In the *Geneva lecture on the symptom*, he makes it clear that 'signification' is a bad translation for *Bedeutung* of the phallus which is, in fact, 'the relation to the Real' (Lacan, 1989, p. 17). Which Real? The Real I just mentioned: the impossibility of gathering together all signifiers at once, the only Real that, strictly speaking, is the effect of language and which the phallic function writes as a function of castration. This latter is not the little story one thinks it is. If we can rely on Lacan's *Ou pire*, castration just is this impossibility. The *parlêtre* is an 'enjoying oneself' – in the absence, of course, of the sexual relationship – unless we say, as Lacan did in *D'un discours qui ne serait pas du semblant*, that speech itself is the sexual relation, an enjoying that still implies castration. In no way is the father convoked in this speech. From the time of *Encore*, speech is the locus of the unconscious as jouissance. 'The unconscious is the fact that being, by speaking, enjoys' (Lacan, 1999, pp. 104–5). More precisely, it is the locus of the *RUCS* (Real Unconscious), insofar as it is not a chain of significations but a 'spoken knowledge', an enjoyed *motérialité* outside meaning. The concept of quilting points would also require rethinking. This is what Lacan begins to do at the end of *Encore*, where he speaks about the One of the swarm of linguistic signifiers subtracted from the knowledge of *lalangue*. The One, this new master signifier, if I may call it that, 'assures the unity, the unity of the subject's copulation with knowledge [. . .] The signifier 'One' is not just any old signifier. It is the signifying order insofar as it is instituted on the basis of the envelopment by which the whole of the chain of signifiers subsists' (Lacan, 1999, p. 143).

The real question Lacan posed was not so much to know if Joyce's art stood in for his phallic position – he takes this as a given – but how: 'How can an art target in an expressly divinatory way the substantialization of the *sinthome*?' (*S*, p. 28). When Lacan evokes 'substance', it is always about jouissance, the only substance with which psychoanalysis deals. That the *sinthome* without the father – which Joyce's art is – restores the Phallus, at once as phallicised ego and as phallic jouissance of the text, so patent in Joyce: this clearly calls into question the phallic function's supposed subordination to the father, so often taken for granted. More specifically, to the father of the metaphor derived from Freud's Oedipus, the one that is summoned up to make sense of filiation beyond that of bodily reproduction, the one Joyce wanted nothing whatsoever to do with.

There is yet another lesson from Joyce that Lacan profited from. Joyce furnished the example that had been missing from his beyond of the Oedipus. There is no question that Joyce enjoyed his *sinthome-name*. But because his *sinthome* repairs in some way the 'slip of the knot', it also restores the knotting of two jouissances: the jouissance of meaning, reduced here to enigma, and phallic jouissance, between Symbolic and Real, that is, wherever he enjoys *lalangue*. From here on, Joyce's success, his Borromean art, obliges us to postulate that these two jouissances are not intrinsically subordinated to the father. As for the jouissance of meaning, we could already find an example in the paranoiac's phantasy, whether of persecution or of redemption. But for phallic jouissance, an example would need to be found, so much had Lacan taught us to think of it as an effect of the paternal function.

What is operative in the *art-dire* (*art-saying*) is speech, with everything this presupposes about the power of the spoken *lalangue* that directs – without the father – the power of this phallic jouissance. Even so, the price is . . . castration. Here again there is a revision to make: castration and speech go together. Certainly castration operates at the sexual level, given that phallic jouissance by itself creates obstacles to the sexual relationship, the Other, the other sex, forever out of reach. I recall Lacan's thesis about *Exiles*. He speaks of it as testimony to the symptom of the sexual non-rapport that Joyce experienced, precisely under Nora's reign. Besides, there is no doubt that, on account of the absence of the sexual relation, '*ab-sexe*', phallic jouissance moves, migrates, transports its power into fields other than the sexual. This is why we sometimes say power is always sexual, but we could just as well say that it never is. But castration, as I have said, operates no less from and at the level of the text that enjoys. We see this in Joyce: his attempts to ward it off right there in the text, most notably in *Finnegans Wake*, which loops back to its beginning from its end, and also in his desire for an uninterrupted reading which never ceases...

Thus, it will have been Joyce who permitted Lacan to validate a step he took – one that received little attention, I believe – a step that consists in undoing the link between the paternal function and the phallic function, which Lacan first posited as necessary and maintained as such until *L'étourdit*. This text must be carefully reread in light of his last elaborations for, while it reaffirms the logical function of the father, he is not the cause of the phallic function. He is only required to constitute into a set the male half of the *sex ratio*.

Put another way, this efficiency ascribed to speech completely revamps it, indeed subverts it, directs it toward the side of the Real, even though in his inaugural text, '*Function and Field of Speech and Language*', Lacan had made the function of speech the very threshold of the Symbolic. Certainly this step was already underway – most notably in *Encore* and in *Joyce le symptôme*, the lecture immediately preceding the seminar on *The Sinthome* – in Lacan's renewal of the concept of the unconscious as a spoken knowledge with its 'home' in *lalangue*, outside meaning, real, and enjoying. But it will have required proof by example, the proof of Joyce's *art-dire*, for the thesis to be confirmed. Contrary to what many have said, including myself in the past, it shows that, for a subject to make up for the deficiency of the father, it takes more than simply renaming oneself. To grasp the inadequacy of this formula, it will be enough to note the following: how many great psychotics in the history of politics, science, and art have renamed themselves, without this having shielded them from madness, without this having made up for the mistake in the Borromean knotting. Joyce did more than rename himself. He gave himself a name, as did many others, but it is name which has a Borromean effect. It is possible to believe that this effect had something to do with the subjective changes that can be perceived in his biography. For example, in the well-attested fact that he who called himself *the artist*, with the definite article to connote his unicity, expressed a sometimes surprising admiration for many other authors, including Hemingway, Gide, d'Annunzio. And equally in the fact that he whose egoism had been so decided, so hardened, became so devoted to his friends, so attentive to their greater and lesser misfortunes. I will not insist any further. Joyce has indeed done without the father, by making use of him. Therefore, a true supplementation by way of the *art-dire*.

Chapter 9
Conclusion

Joyce, beyond the Oedipus

I will begin by returning to the question of diagnosis in Joyce. The assertion of paternal failing, so categorical in *The Sinthome*, has led many a reader of Lacan to think in terms of psychosis. *Mea culpa*, I myself first followed this path (Soler, 2003c), but not without bearing in mind the question of why Lacan, in his seminar and in various other texts on Joyce, so carefully abstained from uttering the word, in spite of emphasising the paternal failing, along with other phenomena consistent with psychosis, most notably in the pages devoted to imposed words and to Joyce's supposedly telepathic daughter (S, p. 79). This could not simply be a matter of consideration for the sensitivities of various readers, especially given that, for Lacan, the term psychosis does not imply any devaluation, in contrast to what we find in the world of psychiatry.

Indeed, as already mentioned, everyone who speaks falls under the blow of the generalised foreclosure of the sexual rapport. On account of this, the diagnostic divisions based on the Name-of-the-Father are, or need to be, modified. Lacan, by introducing the Name-of-the-Father, had ordered, in binary fashion, the entire field of clinical phenomena, with neurosis and perversion on one side, psychosis on the other. Psychosis alone was affected by foreclosure. This binary without nuance still orients numerous clinical texts. But from the moment when the paternal function is perceived to be an obturator for the more radical lack of the sexual relation – Lacan called it an obturator symptom – 'there is Oneness' [*y a d'l'Un*] is no longer reserved to some-ones and is generic to all who speak. 'There is Oneness' would therefore need to be more nuanced and linked to jouissance as well as to saying. This is what Lacan did when he said that 'everyone is delusional', understood as delusional in relation to the phantasy, which plugs up the hole of the impossible relation. Nevertheless, it is not easy to understand this. For the transference – absolutely necessary in psychoanalysis and used to create the signifying chains of meaning – is nothing other than a defence mechanism against the Real and the non-rapport, just like the supplementation symptoms. These are real insofar as their jouissance is outside meaning, fixed in the accidental, contingent encounters of what we call 'life', enduring and implacably resistant to order, yet inscribing what is most unique to the singular identity of each person. This is why psychoanalysis must be thought beyond the Father, as a practice 'oriented towards the Real' (Soler, 2014, p. 61), although it makes use of the Symbolic and the Imaginary. The psychoanalyst's desire must also be desire . . . for the Real. Will it be objected that Lacan, until the end, never stopped speaking about the Name of the Father? True, but this is after he had substituted for the father of the metaphor, inseparable from sex and filiation, the saying father, father because endowed with the power to generate the Borromean knot.

And it was Joyce who provided Lacan with an example – spontaneous, so to speak, non-analytic – that would furnish the support for his thesis of a reinvented psychoanalysis.

At the end of the year devoted to Joyce, he said:

> The hypothesis of the unconscious, and Freud underscores this, is something that can only hold up by presupposing the Name-of-the-Father. Presupposing the Name-of-the-Father, which is certainly God, is how psychoanalysis, when it succeeds, proves that the Name-of-the-Father can just as well be bypassed. One can just as well bypass it on condition that one makes use of it.
>
> (S, p. 116).

This phrase comes after considering the fact that there is no Other of the Other, 'no order of existence' (p. 115) that would be the Other of the Symbolic. A true hole, Lacan says. There follow remarks on saying, on the choice to speak which holds a place of exception in relation to all 'saids' and as the minus-one necessary for constituting them as a set. From here it is easy to formulate the logic of this sentence, which seemed so enigmatic to those who first heard it or read it. The Freudian unconscious, deciphered in what is said by analysands, is 'structured like a language', in other words, it is made from signifiers. But there is no signifier without saying, which is, let us not forget, an act of saying. *Saying*, *dieure*, according to the thesis introduced in *L'étourdit* and taken up again the following year in *Encore*, ex-ists in relation to the signifier. Now, psychoanalysis itself operates through saying. When it succeeds, it allows us to posit a saying beyond all the 'saids' of the analysand, a 'One-saying' that produces unity from their variety. 'This saying that I call back into ex-sistence, this saying that we shouldn't forget, from the primary said, is that which psychoanalysis can claim to close up' (L'é, p. 45). What this presupposes is interpretation adjusted to the structure of discourse, interpretation that does not aim at 'what is said' but to what is 'on the side', the side of enunciation. Therefore, it would be an interpretation that suspends what is true in what is said by the analysand, interpretation that says 'not at all' to utterances of truth. But the analyst says this 'no' not to contradict, deny, or correct; rather to contain, to answer, to throw back. The saying of analysis, the saying that results from two sayings in play – the analyst's, apophantic and oracular, and the analysand's where, in whatever he or she says, there is a demand – this analytic saying, on which Lacan constructed a topology, demonstrates that saying happens very well without a father, and even that the saying is Father. Henceforth, it is indeed possible to affirm that analysis which succeeds does so without the father, precisely in making use of what Lacan called the *Father-saying*. This thesis, announced in 1976 at the very end of the seminar *The Sinthome*, is based on the 1972 formulations in *L'étourdit* that I am briefly evoking here.

Why this time lag? Why only at the end of his exploration of Joyce's case could Lacan formulate it thus? It was because, in 1976, he could authorise himself, implicitly, of course, based on the support furnished by Joyce's *art-dire*, which showed that it was possible to make up for the Name-of-the-Father and, in Joyce's case, to do so without an analysis. We can see Lacan's steps along the way. In 1963, in the first lesson of what would have been a year-long seminar devoted to the Names of the Father (it turned out to be the only lesson, due to his excommunication from the International Psychoanalytical Association), Lacan, with these plural names of the paternal function, was already introducing the notion of possible supplementations. In 1972, *L'étourdit* clarified the nature of the function as a function of saying which is a function of exception, existential in relation to everything that is said. Henceforth, this function is required by the fact of language and that one speaks. In 1976, the *art-dire* of supplementation, by means of which Joyce escapes the 'outside discourse' of psychosis, provides the missing example, necessary to demonstrate the possibility of a discourse that does without the father.

From this I conclude that, if Joyce arrived at his supplementation *sinthome* without recourse to psychoanalysis, it was not without Joyce that Lacan managed to ground his formula for the analytic saying as supplementation.

This in spite of the fact that Lacan had opened the way much earlier, since from *Radiophonie* (Lacan, 1970) on, he had posited that analytic discourse, psychoanalysis, was functioning without recourse to the Name-of-the-Father. Each unconscious is *a* language, but there are several languages, which gives meaning to the phrase 'structured like *a* language' and 'languages fall under the blow of the *pastous* [*not all*] in the most certain way' (L'é, p. 45). Joyce has done as well as any unconscious. He created *his* language, in particular, *lalanglaise* (*lalinglish*), as well as other *lalangues* (S, p. 114). But he did more than that. Through his art, his *savoir-faire*, he restored a place to the language of exception, which ex-ists in relation to spoken languages and conditions the structure of any discourse.

Moreover, from the moment when, to the structure of language, Lacan added the structure of discourses, plural – all of which depend on the place carved out by saying, and wherein *semblants* can came to dwell – he also redefined psychosis. He redefined it as being 'outside discourse', whereas to begin with he had situated only linguistic phenomena there, phenomena that could not be written by his mathemes, $S1$, $S2$, $S.$ a. He left it up to us to know what, in clinical phenomena, signals the *outside discourse*. In the case of Joyce, his *art-dire* corrected what could have been an *outside discourse* by reason of his *de facto foreclosure* of the paternal exception. Thus, in the genealogical tree, he puts himself at the beginning, as I have said, like God himself, homologous to the zero needed to initiate the sequence of whole numbers.

The Real, beyond norms

From Schreber to Joyce, we see the path Lacan travelled. Taking into account, right from the start, the structure of language articulated in speech, he elaborated a progressive construction of the analytic discourse. Function and field, logic and topology, first of language, then of discourse, all have been evoked. We know it only too well, and he was blamed for it by his very own School. Then came the Borromean knot. But reading him today, I note just how propitious these successive excursions were for abolishing some of the more normative starting points.

There is no doubt that for Freud the Oedipus has a normative function, even though not a simple one. Too often it is reduced to what Lacan called the 'little story' concocted in the trio of the conjugal family: daddy, mummy, and me. This is the part so easily popularised, the part that nowadays everyone mouths, including analysands who, upon mentioning father and mother, will explain to us that this is their Oedipus. However, this would be to forget the two texts that meant most to Freud, *Totem and Taboo* and *Moses and Monotheism*. Certainly, one is a myth, the other a historical lucubration, yet the question they pose is not solely about the conformity of sexuation, the child's development into a man or a woman in accordance with his or her sex. It is nothing less than the very possibility, for everyone, of a social link and the Law which conditions this by assuring separation from the primordial object, the mother.

However, with his Oedipus, Freud was in fact legitimising the authority of fathers, instituted well before psychoanalysis and maintained by the institution of the classical, conjugal family, structured as a social link, specifically the link of the Master's discourse. Essentially, it installed an order by way of a *semblant*, a master signifier, S1 – head of the family, the father – in command of his other, the woman-mother, and of his household. Thus it sanctioned the superposition of two couples: the social couple of the parents and the sexual couple of man and woman. It survived at the price of domination, a legalised domination of the wife who, let us not forget, required her husband's permission for all of her social activities. This is why Greek comedy, before the Roman family, invented the idea of the sex strike as the ultimate weapon of those dispossessed of power, namely, women. This type of couple was dismantled in the West in the second half of the twentieth century, as slowly but progressively women were emancipated from their legalised subjection. As a result, the family ceased to be constructed on the model of the Discourse of the Master, and as we can see, when violence occurs, it is not of the 'legalised' kind, but savage. The problem today is not specifically with broken families, but the family in general, which now rests only on private affinities. The family is no longer the basic cell of the social order. It does not prepare its members for adaptation to a principle of order, to a principle of authority that today appears abusive in relation to parity. We forget that to adapt to authority is not simply to submit to it, but also to find the means to resist it, even occasionally to bend it. Lacan made a major statement about this in his article entitled *Les Complexes familiaux* (*Aé*, pp. 23–84).

Today, family support by fathers – as master of the home and spouse – no longer exists. Yet the Oedipal storyline continues to echo this basic social structure at the level of subjective links, by putting the accent on the specifically sexual power of the father as bearer of the phallus, a father who thus orients the identifications and libidinal direction of his descendants. In spite of Freud's attempts to establish the paternal function as a universal, distinct from anthropological variations, it was necessary to conclude, as Lacan finally did, that the Oedipal show could 'not run indefinitely' (É, p. 688), a comment that confirmed its dependency on socio-cultural configurations, something that has now become obvious. A mummy and daddy are not sufficient for there to be this Freudian Oedipus: this Freudian Oedipus with its ratification of two couples who supposedly transmit the sexual order; the child who becomes a man or a woman in accordance with anatomical sex; and more generally, the great Law that prohibits incest for everyone, whatever the sex.

Over time, Lacan spoke out, repeatedly and virulently, against this Oedipus of families, but at the time of the paternal metaphor, it had a different ring to it. We have more or less forgotten about this, due precisely to the acerbic, repeated criticism he later directed toward what he was calling 'the Oedipal ideology'. As an example, in 1972, in *L'étourdit*, he stigmatises the Oedipus as a 'parasitic organism' grafted by Freud onto his own saying of 'no sexual relation'. Lacan then adds:

> .... no easy matter for a cat to find its kittens or for a reader to find meaning.
> The mess is insurmountable, all mixed up in it are castration, the straits in which love engages with incest, the paternal function, the myth wherein the Oedipus duplicates the comedy of the *Père-Orang* (Orang-Father), the perorating Outang.
>
> (Lacan, 1973, p. 13)

And yet, fifteen years earlier, his metaphor was nothing other than the Oedipus arranged like a French garden. With the metaphor, there was no need for recourse to myth or theatre; the elegant paths it laid out replaced both. Lacan thus intended to bring order to the sequels of the Freudian Oedipus for analysts of the time and also remind them of the structural perspective and function of language. The project was a major one and remains so. It was the first step in evaluating just how much we are beings of language and prisoners of its limits. To write his metaphor, Lacan substituted signifiers for the common names of the three persons in the family – father, mother, child – constructing a new trio: the Name-of-the-Father, the Other, and the phallus. Clearly, this was an attempt to begin correcting the Oedipus. Already, this put a stop to the belief that, as soon as the analysand is speaking of daddy, mommy, and me, one has entered the Oedipus. But then the question becomes: does this linguistisation change the expected functions of the Oedipus? It does not.

The linguistic nature of the metaphor neither challenged nor subverted the Oedipus; on the contrary, it justified it symbolically and, on the whole, reinforced it. The metaphor situated the Name-of-the-Father in the place where the human child first encounters signifiers, in the Other, and constituted it as the signifier in the Other which inscribes the Law of the Other. Thus there is an Other of the Other. Lacan himself formulated it in these terms. From then on, the Father appeared as the mediator of the unique signifier of sex, the phallus. Based on this, there is no way to eliminate homologation of the two couples, sexual and familial, through which the Oedipus operates. For sex implies a reproductive function that is socially vested in fathers, that is, until science sweeps it away, which is not happening anytime soon. The metaphor conditioned a discursive link between the sexes, a link where one term governs another, no longer of course through the power of social law, but through the sexual power that comes from the phallus as *semblant*. In fact, Lacan long considered marriage to be something irreducible, the last residue of the degradation of social links. He was wrong about this. It is not the family, but the individual that is the last residue.

Multiple references indicate this explicitly. I am noting only one:

> The Oedipus complex has a normative function, not simply in the subject's moral structure, nor in his relations with reality, but concerning the assumption of his sex [. . .].
>
> The question of genitalization is therefore twofold. There is, on the one hand, growth which carries an evolution or a maturation. There is, on the other hand, in the Oedipus complex, the subject's assumption of his own sex – that is, to call things by their name, what makes it the case that a man assumes the virile type and that a woman assumes a certain feminine type, recognizes herself as a woman and identifies with her functions as a woman. Virility and feminization are the two terms that translate what is essentially the function of the Oedipus complex.
>
> (Lacan, 2017, pp. 149–50)

An even more radical sexual conformism is found in the preceding seminar, *La relation d'objet*. It is not enough for the Oedipal norm to result in heterosexuality; it is also necessary to 'follow the rules' in being heterosexual. The subject, '. . . girl or boy, needs to end up there in such a way that he is correctly situated in relation to the father . . . ' (Lacan, 1998b, p. 201). This means that he or she will be ready to become a father or mother. The Oedipus was thus supposed to direct the Ego Ideal, an ideal both sexual and social, in which case, homosexuality could only be seen as deviance. Moreover, it followed logically – Lacan makes it explicit – that foreclosure of the father in psychosis, beyond the obvious perturbation in the link to reality, inevitably results in anomalies of sexual identification, for example in Freud's Schreber case, the effect known as 'push to the woman'.

The metaphor was thus the royal road to a conformist heterosexuality and a normative relation to reality. In other words, the royal road to mental health and adaptation to the morality of the established social link. At the time, any doubts about these norms did not yet carry weight; and remarks such as we find in Seminars IV and V would not have seemed surprising. Surely this is one of the reasons for their success well beyond the Lacanian community. This doxa was precisely the dominant belief in the IPA (International Psychoanalytic Association) and set the norms for what should logically be expected at the end of an analysis: sexuated love, heterosexual genitality, and the undertaking of procreation. Indeed, the only thing surprising at the time was the attempt at a transposition into linguistic terms, not the fact that the ideological thread remained unchanged, even though Lacan was already emphasising the difference between the Name-of-the-Father as signifier and fathers in reality, a distance that marked the step he took and heralded what was to come in the evolution of his construction.

I insist on this point only to emphasise the extraordinary reversal Lacan came to make in relation to his own original positions. In *L'étourdit*, in 1972, there is almost nothing left of what I am calling the ideological thread. In the meantime, precisely because he had introduced the reference to language – which he never ceased to elaborate – Lacan realised that those who speak suffer less from the Other's norms that vary across cultures than from the real restrictions proper to the logic of language, insurmountable in terms of what they impose as necessary or impossible, never to be transgressed. Hence his formula, in 1969, concerning the analytic act: in the ethics of the act 'it is logic that governs', norms cannot be involved. An end to social norms: this goes without saying. But also an end to sexual norms.

The step beyond the norms that are concerned with the sexuation of beings is, as I have said, inscribed in the now famous formulation presented in *Radiophonie*: 'there is no sexual rapport (Lacan, 1970, p. 65), understood as a relation that could have been stated or written in any discourse. With this step, what beyond norms is left of the Oedipus?

Nothing at all of the sexuating function. The formula 'there is no sexual rapport' says that between the sexes, there is no social link, there is no *semblant* that would have control over the other term. The phallus is certainly a *semblant* but it controls only the comedy of the sexes in the Imaginary, masquerade and parade, nothing of the Real, unless it is castration. No discourse that is not of the *semblant*, and no *semblant* that makes a discourse, a social link between the sexes. Lacan said it in *Télévision*: sexuated love affairs are split from established social links. And—failing to make a discourse—it is in theatres, in literature, or more prosaically, in newspaper articles that affairs of the heart are exhibited, where they end in death or even murder. Outside the theatre, today's families have no way to escape the consequences of the non-rapport. Founded more and more exclusively on the chance meeting of romantic lovers, these families, for this reason, end by being consumed at the core by divisive jouissances. Nor will a child ensure a better foundation for them; we already know this. Moreover, we see that the families which do survive are only those that permit penetration by a master discourse, that is to say, foundations other than love, as is still the case in the great dynasties of industry, finance, and other forms of power; or in countries where a harsher patriarchy reigns supreme, with religion as a support.

We must therefore rethink things from the perspective of a generalised foreclosure of the sexual relation. In our civilisation, there is no longer any established discourse to stand in for it, such as King and Queen, Knight and Lady. This is finished. Now, equality obligates. What remains, then, if not the singular symptoms by which each of us could bond – possibly, not necessarily – to the other sex? Lacan finishes by saying that a woman, for a man, is a symptom. But this is only a specific case; every partner is a symptom. But a symptom is always singular, one by one; and, in the absence of the sexual relation, there may be a wide variety of supplementation symptoms that are capable of creating a relation to a partner, whether male or female. As a result, Lacan realised that his Oedipal metaphor was itself the formula for a symptom, one among others, nothing more. And he said it: the Oedipus is a symptom, the Oedipal father is a symptom. I would point out that it is a dated symptom. We can see this in the evolution of our times, which in some way indicates that it belonged to a time when the family held, a symptom typical of a given social order, that is to say, one among other possibilities. This thesis of a supplementation symptom, a symptom that makes up for the foreclosure of the sexual relation – Lacan established it against himself, against his metaphor, against his own comments. As support for my statement, I quote Lacan: ' . . . the analyst is just as liable as anyone else to have a bias regarding sex, above and beyond what the unconscious reveals to him' (É, p. 615).

To the formula 'no sexual rapport', we must, of course, add the formulas of sexuation. These attempt to effect a correspondence between the *sex ratio*, that is to say, the anatomical, biologically reproductive couple, and the couple of desire and jouissance, by apportioning the two sexes in relation to the unique function of the phallus. But the following year, in *Encore*, Lacan went one step further. He said of those who speak: they have a choice to be on one side or the other (Lacan, 1999, p. 71). This means, first of all, that anatomy is not destiny, something we have known for a very long time and without needing to go through psychoanalysis. I note, however, that if there is choice, then the correspondence between the *all phallic/not all phallic* and the *sex ratio* – what these formulas known as the formulas of sexuation were attempting to establish – is called into question. Lacan said even more about sexuated beings: they authorise themselves. In other words, they are not authorised either by bodily anatomy or by the Other of the Symbolic. This is the polar opposite of normative sexuality, the effects expected from the metaphor. And if they do authorise themselves, how? Linguistic castration is for everyone who speaks. That leaves only body events, the symptoms that are an answer to it, jouissance symptoms, whether *all* or *not all* phallic. The result is that the couple, hetero or otherwise, is no longer attached to an order. And while there is a choice of *all/not all* in the castration function, which is the phallic function, *parlêtres* do not have a choice regarding the *motérialité* of their unconscious which, through contingencies, creates *fixions* of their symptomatic jouissance. Let us also remember that Lacan, in attributing to Freud the saying 'there is no sexual rapport', is situating it as a 'subversion', a subversion whose foundation he will have demonstrated to be Real, that is, an impossibility programmed by the structure of language, compensated for by another Real, more contingent and always singular, that of the symptom event. With this, it is hardly excessive to say that Lacan has constructed a theoretical economy that is not subjective but sexual.

Nevertheless, as I said above, the function of the Oedipus was not solely sexual but also subjectivising. By way of the identifications that it supposedly controlled, it assured – as Lacan pointed out in his *Note on the Child* (Lacan, 1990b, p. 8) – the 'transmission of a subjective constitution'. Indeed, Lacan's *R Schema*, which may be found in '*On a Question Prior to Any Possible Treatment of Psychosis*' and is contemporary with his paternal metaphor, clearly seeks to specify the foundations of that subject for whom the Father is called to account. Subjective constitution is something altogether different from constitution of the sexual symptom.

Lacan never lost sight of this. Having challenged his theory of the paternal metaphor and evoked the plural Names-of-the-Father, Lacan – always logical – began to explore not so much the Name-of-the-Father – 'a Name to lose' – but symptomatic fathers, one by one; and it was then, in the lesson of 21 January 1975 of the seminar *R.S.I.*, that he put forward the notion of a father-symptom, one who takes 'paternal care' of his children.

Paternal care: here is something new in Lacan's writing. It is not my impression that he was inviting 'daddies', as we call them today, to compete for what, for a very long time, belonged exclusively to women, though not necessarily to mothers, since the elite used to turn over so-called 'maternal care' to wet nurses. Today, many new fathers boast about entering the nursery, and some are asked to do so in the name of equality. Many consider themselves to be better fathers the more they try to be like the other, the mothers. They are free to do so, if this is their cup of tea. We have no reason to think it harmful. If 'maternal care' is care of the body in conjunction with transmission of *lalangue* and discourse, there is no one naturally in charge of this. The problem is elsewhere. It does not have to do with birth or survival or even entry into the bath of language. It is, rather, a problem of the transmission of the basis for identity.

This paternal care by a symptom father is no doubt to be sought on the side of the father who names, the one Lacan emphasises at the end of *The Sinthome*, the one from whom one may expect a saying of nomination, as index of and condition for a desire that is not anonymous. This is a major change in relation to the metaphor, for nomination is a *saying* and *saying* does not come from the Other; it does not come from the Symbolic. It is an existential function which has an effect in structure but is not itself a fact of structure. And what is existential is Real, a contingent event.

With the Father of the name, Lacan has inscribed a new disjunction between the father function and fathers. Today, we find all kinds of fathers: present, absent, more motherly than the mother, loving, hateful, problematic, vigilant, negligent, not to forget jouissance fathers, by which I mean those who are abusive. In brief, fathers as various and diverse as the individual '*unarities*' of our time. Already, analytic literature is having a field day drawing up this collection of portraits. But a collection does not a clinic make. Instead, the question to be asked in each clinical case is: what is the jouissance symptom that makes up for the foreclosure of the sexual relation? And regarding 'subjective constitution', which is separate from sexual constitution, is there a father of the Name and, if not, is there a supplementation?

Naming seems to be an act. Much has been said about it in relation to the father, the one who is there to respond, which also means that he makes himself 'response-able'. Certainly, this is of great importance, but what is the phenomenology? It does not correspond to any before or after of the act. And it is different from what happens in the Bible with objects and animals, whose nomination is performative, since they have nothing to say in reply. But for those who speak, the name that is given has no effect unless it is received, accepted, not refused. Thus the one who is named has a part in his or her own naming. There is no name without reception of the name. Naming Joyce *the symptom*, Lacan immediately added: I believe he would have accepted it. There is no self-naming; and only insults attempt to name by force – in vain – for hurting is not naming. The insult qualifies, negatively. The name, on the other hand, indexes, without qualifying. In this sense, unlike 'naming to', giving a name is never prescriptive. According to Russell, it is at most descriptive.

We can thus see, at the end of Lacan's teaching, the evolution beyond norms of the two functions originally attributed to the Oedipal metaphor. The sexuating function becomes the supplementation symptom of the non-relation; it does not pass through the mediation of the Other. The paternal function decides neither the inscription on one side or the other of the formulas of sexuation, nor the fixation, in early infancy, of the 'jouissance event'. The symptom 'comes from the Real'. Moreover, it is of the Real, not of the Symbolic; the sexual is not transmitted. As for the function of identification, what remains is nomination. Also an event, it is different from the 'jouissance event'. But what the two events have in common is that both fall under the *Tuchè*. And this nomination is not the privilege of fathers. On the contrary, it is nomination that is father. Put another way, the important thing to see in Lacan's last teachings is not so much that fathers are symptoms. The important thing is that the paternal function itself is an existential symptom, not a jouissance symptom, but a *saying sinthome*, the fourth in the Borromean knot, which can make it possible for the three other consistencies to hold together. The point is that reduction of this function to the contingency of an event makes it precarious, puts it at the mercy of the encounter, just like love, putting it simultaneously at odds with marriage – which is self-evident – and also with sex – which requires demonstration.

Those who protest against gay marriage say that a child needs both a mother and a father, who are man and woman. The subtext is that the child should grow up to be just like them and start a family. We could say: what the child needs is only a desire that is not anonymous, from which to choose his or her own life and pathways. Yet we need to bear in mind that this desire is not wholly sufficient. At the end, Lacan said: You are all miscarriages of the desire of the Other. The formula makes quite an impression, but what it says is something very precise: the desire of the Other, whether or not there is a father, whether or not there is a nomination, cannot take you to term, the very definition of miscarriage. It can bring you into the world, even assure you of the conditions for a subjective position compatible with reality and the social link, but it will not take you as far as the sexuated couple; only the symptom will supplement . . . possibly, but not necessarily.

Which amounts to saying that Lacan's teaching, in its last elaborations, makes it clear that, contrary to the original postulate of psychoanalysis, 'subjective constitution' and the sexual economy of jouissance, the two economies that the Oedipus sought to join, do not walk the same path nor follow the same rules.

Names of the Reals

One may ask about the dominance of the Name and what it was that pushed Lacan toward the Father of the Name. There is nothing in *L'étourdit* that heralds this. With reference to set theory, *L'étourdit* situated *saying* as an exception, logically existing in relation to the sayings of truth. From then on, it was to be defined as a 'saying no' [*dire que non*] to the register of truth, the half-said. From there, it was possible to conceive an interpretation that uses equivocation, and in this way says 'no' to the 'what is said' of truth, targeting instead the *saying*. From the exception that is the *saying* of 'no' to the 'saids' of truth, the Father was rethought as a specific exception, not to the 'saids' of truth but to the phallic function itself. With this exception, Lacan was revealing the implicit logic that sustained, without Freud's knowing it, the neurotic delusion of the Father of the Primal Horde, the father credited with an impossible jouissance, of which all of his sons were deprived. Based on this logical foundation, Lacan hoped to devalue the myth of the supposedly castrating father; for as far as fathers are concerned – he said it categorically – they are castrated just like everyone who speaks. *Saying* ex-ists in relation to language and therefore it also ex-ists in relation to logic, but the *saying of the name* has a different import. How is it imposed or invoked? I see no other answer except by a Real – and this is quite topical.

Alain Badiou hit the nail on the head when he said: 'Of what is Sarkozy the name?' Wonderful! It has become a syntagm used all over the media:

'Of what is *x* the name?' This is not a question one asks about a signifier which, of course, signifies a subject, but produces only a signified and thus misses the referent, the Real. The Real: whatever it is, it is not One. The Real which is not narrated, but subsists outside narrative, outside the stories of which I spoke, this Real can be indexed by a name, and is moreover, quintessentially, what there is to name. The referent that the signifier misses is what the Name pins down. From this, we understand the requirement for a Name, all the more so as *semblants* get depleted and fail to pacify the Real. It is no accident that today we are seeing an upsurge in the demand to name everything we do not know how to explain, resulting in an unbridled taxonomy, particularly in the field of mental health. Today this is also happening quite clearly with sexuality. The traditional order having run out of steam, sexuality has now been reduced to the material presence of singular, very real symptoms that belong to the order of the One outside meaning, that is, to the One of the autistic letter, or to the Borromean One that knots together diverse jouissances. Thus we now see an urgent need for admission, together with civil and social recognition, of these symptom names: gay, bi, trans. This is because only the Name can fasten a Real to the linguistic order. The proof is in the myth: God names what he has created.

The real of jouissance is 'contradictory to every verisimilitude' (Aé, p. 374). With the real of symptoms, we are in the logic of the generalised 'not all', something alarming for us because symptoms do not provide an order of jouissances. On the contrary, this Real is, essentially, dis-order, the very opposite of what is aimed at by science. Whence anxiety, the affect typical for any advent of the Real. What then remains – this is Lacan's thesis – is segregation and the logic of camps to separate out all the differences between symptomatic *unarities*, or to attenuate the fight between equivalents, for the Real of jouissance symptoms lacks any order. '*There is Oneness*' [*Y a d'l'Un*] and nothing else at this level, apart from the *One-saying*, which knows it is the One and only (Lacan, 2011, p. 243). Nevertheless, as Lacan says in 1977, there is hatred, the affect that responds to intolerable differences. I have already commented on this (Soler, 2011). It seems to be on the increase everywhere today, in households, couples, schools, neighbourhoods, etc., accelerated by the effects of capitalism.

We might then be tempted to think that the Oedipus of our grandfathers was basically a good symptom which, by bringing together the links of family and sex, brought order, obviously at the price of the domination of women. But is it possible to organise the various symptomatic solutions into a hierarchy by anything other than personal preferences, which are themselves symptoms? Today, those born from this old symptom – no doubt there are still many – remain rooted in their fathers and tend to prefer this symptom, out of which they have been constituted and moulded. Indeed, I believe this was the case for Lacan himself; there are many indications. But lest we give in to prejudgment, let us not forget the literature of indignation that was produced in the wake of its damage over preceding centuries; let us recall that the Oedipal symptom did not protect against misfortune, violence, or even psychosis. Above all, yes, above all, let us not forget that the position of the psychoanalyst must exclude the refusal of what is imposed as Real. For the Real, both that of the subject and that of sex, is the psychoanalyt's responsibility. Also, let us not forget Joyce and his *art-dieure* (*art-saying*) of the Borromean name, without the father. From the negativism of no-saying, his *Nego* to paternal norms, Joyce moved to the Name of exception. As for Lacan – by moving from the logic of 'no-saying' to the Father of the Name, at the very moment when he recognised the unordered Real of symptoms – he was in fact confirming the superiority of the Name over the *semblant*. I have emphasised the heterogeneity of the jouissance event in the body and the nomination event of *saying*. But the Name knots these together. Not only does it not prescribe, but its operation, beyond any norm, fastens a Real that is material and unexpected to the field of discourse. In this way, it makes the singular Real of the symptom enter into a social link – something that will be more and more necessary.

I thus conclude by reiterating how very important it is for psychoanalysts to stay in touch with their own times, and by this I mean to be free of old categories, not in order to give way to fashions driven by the marketplace, but simply to be able to respond – as analysts – to those addressing them at the beginning of this century.

Bibliography

Aubert, J. (1982). *Œuvres*, vol. 1, 1901–1915. Trans. Jacques Aubert, Jacques Borel, Jenny S. Bradley, André Du Bouchet, Élisabeth Janvier, Anne Machet, Ludmilla Savitzky and Marie Tadié. Édition de Jacques Aubert, Paris: Gallimard. Paris: Gallimard.
Ellmann, R. (1982). *James Joyce* (Oxford Lives). Oxford: Oxford University Press.
Ellmann, R. (2003). *Selected Letters of James Joyce*. London: Faber & Faber. (SL)
Freud, S. (1909) Three Essays on the Theory of Sexuality. *The Standard Edition of the Complete Psychological Works of Sigmund Freud, Vol. VII*. London: The Hogarth Press.
Freud, S. (1961)[1907]. Letter from Sigmund Freud to The Family, 22 September 1907. *Letters of Sigmund Freud 1873–1939*. London: Hogarth Press, pp. 261–3.
Freud, S. (1936). *A Disturbance of Memory on the Acropolis*. Standard Edition (Vol. 22), London: Hogarth Press, pp. 237–48.
Joyce, J. (1963). *Stephen Hero: A Part of the First Draft of A Portrait of the Artist as a Young Man*. New York City, NY: New Directions Publishing. (SH)
Joyce, J. (1992). *A Portrait of the Artist as a Young Man*. Ware: Wordsworth Classics. (*PAYM*)
Joyce, J. (2010). *Ulysses*. Ware: Wordsworth Classics.
Lacan, J. (1968). Proposition du 9 octobre 1967 sur le psychanalyste de l'Ecole. *Scilicet*, 1: 14–30.
Lacan, J. (1970). Radiophonie. *Scilicet*, 2/3. Paris: Seuil.
Lacan, J. (1973). L'étourdit. *Scilicet*, 4. Paris: Seuil. (*L'é*)
Lacan, J. (1973/1974). *Le Séminaire, Livre XXI: Les non-dupes errent*. Unpublished. (NDE)
Lacan, J. (1975a). *De la psychose paranoïaque dans ses rapports avec la personalité*. Paris: Seuil.
Lacan, J. (1975b). *Le Séminaire. Livre XXII: R.S.I.* Unpublished. (R.S.I.)
Lacan, J. (1975c). La Troisième, Intervention au Congrès de Rome. *Lettres de l'école freudienne*, 16: 177–203.

Lacan, J. (1976). Conférences et entretiens dans les Universités nord-américaines. *Scilicet*, 6/7. Paris: Seuil.

Lacan, J. (1979). Journal d'Ornicar? *Ornicar?*, 17–18, p. 278.

Lacan, J. (1989). Geneva Lecture on the Symptom (1975). *Analysis*, 1: 7–26.

Lacan, J. (1990a)[1973]. *Television: A Challenge to the Psychoanalytic Establishment*. New York: W.W. Norton & Co.

Lacan, J. (1990b) (trans. R. Grigg). Note on the Child. *Analysis*, No. 2: 7–8.

Lacan, J. (1998a). *The Seminar of Jacques Lacan, Book XI: The Four Fundamental Concepts of Psychoanalysis* (1964). New York: W.W. Norton & Co.

Lacan, J. (1998b). *Le Séminaire, Livre IV: La Relation d'objet*. Paris: Seuil.

Lacan, J. (1999). *The Seminar of Jacques Lacan, Book XX: Encore. On Feminine Sexuality, The Limits of Love and Knowledge (1972–1973)*. New York: W.W. Norton & Co.

Lacan, J. (2001). *Autres écrits*. Paris: Seuil. (*Aé*)

Lacan, J. (2005). *Écrits*. New York: W.W. Norton & Co. (*É*)

Lacan, J. (2011). *Le Séminaire, Livre XIX: . . . ou pire*. Paris: Seuil.

Lacan, J. (2012). *Postface to the French Edition of Seminar XI*. Hurly Burly, 7, pp. 17–21.

Lacan, J. (2016). *The Seminar of Jacques Lacan, Book XXIII: The Sinthome* (ed. Jacques-Alain Miller, trans. Adrian Price). Cambridge: Polity Press. (*S*)

Lacan, J. (2017). *The Seminar of Jacques Lacan, Book V: Formations of the Unconscious* (ed. Jacques-Alain Miller, trans. Russell Grigg) Cambridge: Polity Press.

Lacan, J. and Aubert, J. (1987). *Joyce avec Lacan*. Paris: Navarin. (*J/L*)

Scholes, R.E. and Kain, R.M. (1965). *The workshop of Daedalus: James Joyce and the raw materials for A Portrait of the Artist as a Young Man*. Evanston, IL: Northwestern University Press.

Soler, C. (1999). *L'ombilic et la chose*. Presentation for the Centenary of the Interpretation of Dreams, 30 May 1999, Espace Analytique, Paris.

Soler, C. (2001). *L'Aventure littéraire, ou la psychose inspirée, Rousseau, Joyce, Pessoa*. Paris: Champ lacanien.

Soler, C. (2003a). *Ce que Lacan disait des femmes*. Paris: Champ lacanien.

Soler, C. (2003b). Les phénomènes perceptifs du sujet. In: *L'Inconscient à ciel ouvert de la psychose*. Toulouse: Presses universitaires du Mirail.

Soler, C. (2003c). *L'Inconscient à ciel ouvert de la psychose*. Toulouse: Presses universitaires du Mirail.

Soler, C. (2003–2004). *La Querelle des diagnostics*. Documents du Champ lacanien. Unpublished.

Soler, C. (2011). *Les Affects lacaniens*. Paris: PUF.

Soler, C. (2013). *Ce qui reste de l'enfance*. Paris: Champ lacanien.

Soler, C. (2014). *Lacan: The Unconscious Reinvented*. Trans. Esther Faye and Susan Schwartz. London: Karnac Books.

Index

aesthetic theory 81, 82
'Agency of the Letter in the Unconscious, The' (Lacan) 65
Aimée case 16
all phallic/not all phallic 120, 122
analysis *see* psychoanalysis
analysts *see* psychoanalysts
a-normale-ity 64–6
Aristotle 84
art-dieure 125
art-dire 104, 108, 109, 110, 113, 114
astonishment 76
attribution, subjective 83
Aubert, Jacques 2, 21, 40, 43, 80, 81, 83, 98
automatism, mental 81

Badiou, Alain 123
Befriedigung 76
Bejahung 45
body: 'civilized' 59; connection with language 59–60; erotic use of 58; hysteric use of 58; of Joyce 57–8
Borromean art 73, 86, 88, 101, 104, 108
Borromean clinic 3
Borromean consistency 18
Borromean Father 18
Borromean knot: and the Father function 53, 112; fourth element of 122; function of 2, 4, 86, 91, 99; of the Imaginary 72; and jouissance 17, 20, 124; in Joyce's writings 73, 86, 88, 101, 108–9, 125; Lacan's references to 1, 2, 4, 15, 16, 18, 25, 40, 114; in psychoanalysis 18; relationship between Symbolic and Imaginary 41–2, 76, 105; three-ringed 18, 24, 72–3, 105; *see also* Imaginary; Real; Symbolic
Borromean name 125
Borromean One 25, 124
British Imperialism 86

capitalism 65, 124
Carco, Francis 39
castration 58, 93, 105, 107–9, 116, 119, 123; linguistic 120
Catholic Church 31, 32, 86; Joyce's aversion to 29–30
Chamber Music (Joyce) 77
Church 31; *see also* Catholic Church
claritas 22, 84, 92
common sense 60, 73, 74, 75
compromise formation 12
Cooper, David Graham 51
cynicism 98

Das Kapital (Marx) 30
de-epiphanisation 84
delusion 9, 15, 17, 40, 41, 42, 111, 123
deo-logue 42, 43, 98, 103
depression 29
Derrida, Jacques 1
Descartes, René 76
Dieue-père 43
dieure-le-père 43
Disturbance of Memory on the Acropolis, A (Freud) 29
dream analysis 95, 97, 98
Dubliners (Joyce) 77
Duchamp, Marcel 84
Duras, Marguerite 4

Eastman, Max 98
Eckhart, Meister 42, 43, 103
Ego 54–6, 70, 92; corrective 72; of enigma 97; as Imaginary 72; connecting Imaginary and Symbolic 72–3
Ego Ideal 117
egoism 56, 110
elementary phenomena 16, 81
ellipses 15, 83
Ellmann, Richard 29, 46, 98
Encore (Lacan) 20, 84, 107, 112
enigma: in dream analysis 95; ego of 97; of enunciation 50, 79, 87, 89, 98; in *Epiphanies* 81–2, 83, 85; false 87; in *Finnegans Wake* 77–9, 85, 88, 89, 91, 93; in Joyce's art 5, 22, 25, 33, 86–8, 90, 96–9, 105, 108, 112; Lacan's references to 14, 15; in *Portrait of the Artist as a Young Man* 88, 91; saying of 91; in *Stephen Hero* 88
Enigma-name 86, 88, 89, 90, 91, 93, 105
enunciation 15, 79, 86, 113; enigma of 50, 79, 87, 89, 98; and phonation 90
epiphanies 80–6; ambiguity of 85
Epiphanies (Joyce) 80, 81–2, 83, 85, 86
epiphanisation 84
equivocations 1, 22, 36, 61–3, 78, 87, 89, 98, 123; multi-linguistic 74; pulverulence of 73–7
erogenous zones 58
Eros 13–14
eroticism 67, 68, 106
Exiles (Joyce) 68, 91, 109

family history 5, 44
family novels 9
family romance 5, 7
father(s): Borromean 18; castrating 123; diverse manifestations of 121; failure of 44, 45–6, 49, 111; function of 122; as *mi-dieure* 48; and paternal care 47; as signifier of the Law 45–6; as symptom 14, 16, 121, 125; *see also* father-symptom; Joyce, John; *pére-sinthome*; *pére-version*; *symptome-Pére*
father metaphor 108; *see also* metaphor
Father of the Name 65
Father of the Primal Horde 123
Father-saying 113

father-symptom 48, 67, 121; *see also père-sinthome*
feminization 117
Finnegans Wake (Joyce) 4, 22, 25, 51, 73, 74, 80, 86–8, 92, 97, 104, 106, 109; enigma in 77–9, 85, 88, 89, 91, 93; equivocations in 75
foreclosure 111, 118; *de facto* 49–52, 53, 65–6, 71, 114; of the sexual revolution 119
Foucault, Michel 39, 48
fragments 79, 81–4, 87
free association 1, 2, 16, 17, 86
Freud, Sigmund: and *Befriedigung* 76; and *Bejahung* 45; on delusion 41, 123; and deo-logue 43; on desire 61–2; on dream analysis 95, 97; on jouissance 16, 63; love of Rome 26, 27, 29, 30; named cases of 12, 39; on narcissism 66; novel of 7–10; on the Other 50; on psychoanalysis 1, 4, 5, 7, 11, 20, 61–2, 66, 74, 112; Schreiber case 15, 41, 42, 45, 48, 58, 64, 105, 106, 114, 118; on sexual meaning 11–12; on sexual rapport 120; *see also* Oedipus complex
Freud, Sigmund (writings): *A Disturbance of Memory on the Acropolis* 29; *Moses and Monotheism* 115; *Three Essays on the Theory of Sexuality* 11; *Totem and Taboo* 9, 115
'Function and the Field of Speech and Language' 109

Galvani, Luigi 84
genital drive 13–14
glove reference 68–9
God 103, 112, 114, 124; *see also* God-the-Father; Name-of-the-Father
God-the-Father 43
Gorog, Françoise 49
Grammar of Assent (Newman) 61

half-saying (*mi-dire*) 48, 49
hallucinations 17, 81, 83
having/being alternative 64
heresy 21, 25, 35, 36
hermeneutics 5
heterosexuality 11, 64, 118
holophrastic discourse 17
homosexuality 117–18; and marriage 122–3

hysterics 58–9
hystoire 9

identification, sexual 64, 118
identity: establishment of 15, 88, 112, 121; phonatory 85, 104; sexual 64
Imaginary: of the body 24, 54, 57, 69, 72, 99; connection with Symbolic 8, 16, 17, 40, 41, 58, 59, 73, 76, 95, 96, 104–5, 107, 112; in default 54–7; Ego as 72; eroticism of 106, 119; function of 68; in Joyce's writings 42, 79, 85, 86, 88; knotting of 72, 76; as one of three consistencies 14, 16, 17, 101, 105; Real disconnected from 8, 16, 17, 43; relationship with the Other 41; restoration of 42; substitutive 97; unknotting of 53–9, 70, 79, 105; and unworthy fathers 45; *see also* Borromean knot
imperialism, British 86
incest 64, 116
induction 41
International Psychoanalytic Association (IPA) 118
Ireland 31

jaculation-phonation 90
James Joyce International Symposium 2
Jésus la caille (Carco) 39
joui-sense 17, 24, 73, 74, 76, 77, 94, 98, 105
jouissance: autistic 73, 97; of the body 20, 58, 59, 67–8; and desire 62; distancing 95; diverse 124; divisive 119; fixing of 12, 13, 16, 74, 75, 79; God's 103; heterogeneity of 125; and language 62–3, 83, 97; of meaning 108; opaque 16, 79, 91, 94, 96, 97, 98; ordering of 75; original sin of 23; and the Other 102–3; paternal 14, 48, 121, 123; phallic 17, 105–6, 108–9, 120; power of 106; and psychoanalysis 108; Real of 2, 17, 19, 43, 58, 95, 96, 98, 112, 124; repressed 12–13; sexual 10, 11, 12, 13, 105, 111, 120, 123; in sinthome 14, 17, 24, 108; of speech 87, 106, 107; substitutive 11; surplus of 99; symptomatic 13, 16, 39, 47, 48, 68, 70, 74, 83, 96, 99, 120, 121; of the symptom-letter 17, 22, 24, 69,

79, 91, 94, 97, 98; and *Thanatos* 16; and the three consistencies 17, 105; transgressive 48, 49, 53; in the writings of James Joyce 26, 77, 80, 97, 98, 103; see also *joui-sense*
jouissance event 20, 58, 122, 125
Joyce, Giorgio 26, 28, 67, 69
Joyce, James: aesthetic theory of 81, 82; as *the artist* 36, 110; aversion to the Catholic Church 29–30; on Christianity 30–4; education with the Jesuits 26, 45–7, 49, 93; use of enigma in writing 86–8, 90, 96, 97, 98, 99, 105, 108, 112; identification of his writing with awakening 96; intellectual strike 31; and the Name 125; praxis of 102–4; relationship to his own body 53–9; relationship with Nora 53, 63–4, 66–70; in Rome 26–30; as self-made man 43; success as a writer 92–4; as symptom 5, 15, 21, 39, 66, 122; and the unconscious 75, 103; unreadability of 77–80
Joyce, James (writings): *Chamber Music* 77; *Dubliners* 77; *Epiphanies* 80, 81–2, 85, 86; *Exiles* 68, 91, 109; *Finnegans Wake* 4, 22, 25, 51, 73, 74, 75, 77–80, 85, 86–8, 91, 92, 97, 104, 106, 109; *A Portrait of the Artist as a Young Man* 3, 25, 35, 41, 51, 54, 59, 60, 71, 77, 84, 88, 91, 103; *Stephen Hero* 25, 33, 41, 46, 60, 75, 77, 88, 91, 103; *Ulysses* 1, 22, 36, 51–2, 76, 77, 78–9; *The Villanelle of the Temptress* 82
Joyce, John 43–4, 46, 49, 51–2
Joyce, Lucia 67
Joyce, Nora 4, 26, 27, 28, 29, 30, 93; as Imaginary extra 70; as inside-out glove 69; relationship with James 53, 63–4, 66–70
Joyce, Stanislaus 26, 28, 46, 49, 73, 77, 81, 94, 96; *My Brother's Keeper* 47
Joyce avec Lacan (ed. Aubert) 21
Joyce le symptôme II (Lacan) 21, 34, 96
Jung, Carl G. 76, 79, 94

Kant, Immanuel 55, 69
know-how 3, 86; of the artist 85, 101; vs. knowledge 102; *see also* savoir-faire
knowledge: vs. know-how 102; spoken 108; unconscious 62

Lacan, Jacques: analysis of Joyce 3, 98; on the analytic experience 2; on *Exiles* 109; on the ideal of the Other 34; on Joyce's writing style 87–8; on paternal failing 44–5; rewriting the Oedipus myth 9
Lacan, Jacques (lectures): *Geneva lecture on the symptom* 19, 107; Yale University (1975) 19
Lacan, Jacques (seminars): *Seminar IV: La relation d'objet* 65, 117, 118; *Seminar V: Les formations de l'inconscient* 118; *Seminar X: L'angoisse (Anxiety)* 9, 47; *Seminar XI: Les quatre concepts fondamentaux* 2; *Seminar XIV: La logique du fantasme* 8, 98; *Seminar XVIII: D'un discours qui ne serait pas du semblant* 92; *Seminar XX: Encore* 20, 84, 107, 112; *Seminar XXI: Les non-dupes errent* 18, 47, 102; *Seminar XXII: R.S.I.* (Real, Symbolic, Imaginary) 2, 13, 14, 15–18, 45, 47, 63, 74, 121; *Seminar XXIII: Le sinthome* 1, 2–3, 4, 7, 14, 21–2, 34, 39–40, 46, 73, 74, 85, 101, 102, 111, 113, 121
Lacan, Jacques (writings): 'The Agency of the Letter in the Unconscious' 65; 'Function and the Field of Speech and Language' 109; *Joyce le symptôme II* 21, 34, 96; *Les Complexes familiaux* 115; *L'étourdit* 64, 74, 104, 105, 109, 112, 113, 118, 123; *Note on the Child* 120; 'On a Question Prior to Any Possible Treatment of Psychosis' 15, 41, 45, 80, 120; *Radiophonie* 114, 118; *Télévision* 17, 119
lalanglaise (lalinglish) 114
lalangue: effect of on bodies 19; individual choice of 31, 63; and jouissance 74, 94, 97, 108; Joyce's use of 23, 32, 39, 60–1, 62, 63, 75, 78, 79, 85–6, 88, 98–9, 102, 108, 114; Lacan's use of 62, 108–9; maternal 19, 60, 62; paternal 121; and phonation 89; Real of 19; signifiers from 24; as the spoken language of the unconscious 18, 83, 106
La Logique du phantasme seminar 8, 98
La relation d'objet seminar 65, 117
Les Complexes familiaux (Lacan) 115

Les non-dupes errent seminar 18, 47, 102
L'étourdit (Lacan) 64, 74, 104, 105, 109, 112, 113, 118, 123
letter-fixion 98
letters: agency of 22, 25, 37n3; autistic 124; function of 69; and jouissance 12–13, 17, 22, 24, 62–3, 69, 97, 98; and lalangue 99; materiality of 76–7; pure 25, 61, 86; Real of 2, 76, 91; as signifier 13; symptom- 17, 25; of the unconscious 1, 24, 69; unreadable 75, 77–80, 88; as waste 23, 94
letters (postal): from Freud to family 27; from James to his aunt 67; between James and Nora 63, 66–7, 69; from James to Stanislaus 26, 28, 30, 31
linguistic crystal 13
literary criticism 5, 94
literary critics 76–7
literary fiction 5
literary symptoms 73
literature 5
Little Hans 65
logic 34–6
logorrhoea 17
LOM 25

man/woman alternative 64
marriage 117, 122; gay 122–3
Marx, Karl 30
maternal care 121
metaphor 78, 108, 116–17, 118; father 108; Oedipal 119, 122; paternal 44–5, 64, 65, 107, 116, 120–1
metonymy 78
Miller, Jacques-Alain 22
Millot, Catherine 83
Moses 42, 43, 103
Moses and Monotheism (Freud) 115
My Brother's Keeper (S. Joyce) 47

Name of exception 125
Name-of-the-enigma 86, 88, 89, 90, 91, 93, 105
Name-of-the-Father 17, 43, 44, 45, 47, 50, 51, 64, 102, 111–14, 113, 116–17, 118, 121
Names of the father 65
naming 122
narcissism 56, 57–8, 66, 67, 98
narcynicism 98

narrative: abolition of 98; of the dream 95; existence of the Real outside of 124; limits of 9; linguistic 8; and the truth 8–9; vector of a novel 78
negationist position 25
negativism 32, 125
'Nego' 25–6, 84, 98; becoming act 71–2; Joyce in Rome 26–30; Joyce on Christianity 30–4; Joyce's strike 31–2, 36; to paternal norms 125
neo-world 79
neurosis 10, 40, 111
Newman, John Henry 61
nomination 71–2, 122; by God 124
normality 48
Note on the Child (Lacan) 120

obturator symptom 111
Oedipal metaphor 119, 122
Oedipal solution 64, 68
Oedipal symptom 125
Oedipus complex: beyond 7, 101, 108; Freud's version of 7, 9, 13, 21, 36, 47, 64, 108, 114–16; function of 64, 120, 124; Joyce's refutation of 36; Lacan's version of 7, 9, 36, 44, 47, 64, 116–19, 123; as symptom 119
Oedipus story/myth 9, 17, 95
'On a Queston Prior to Any Possible Treatment of Psychosis' (Lacan) 15, 41, 45, 80, 120
Oneness 35, 111, 124
Ornicar? (journal) 21, 22
Other 11, 33, 116–17; belief in 40; desire of 123; divine 34; Joyce's affection for 98; Law of 50, 117; mediation of 122; norms of 118; of the Other 102, 103, 112; as place 50; rejection of 52, 57; signifier of 50; subject's need for 42; of the Symbolic 112, 120
over-determination 12

paranoia 78, 108
parlêtre 18, 20, 58, 63, 75, 106, 107, 120
passions 72–3, 76
pastiche 5, 22, 43, 78
paternal care 14, 47, 121
paternal metaphor 44–5, 64, 65, 107, 116, 120–1
pathological 55
perception 80

père-sinthome 16, 17, 18, 40, 48, 49, 67
père-version 14, 15, 47, 48, 49, 68
perversion 2, 53, 63, 83, 111
phallus 116, 117; alternative to 64; *Bedeutung* of the 107; difference of 69; function of 104–7, 109, 120, 123; and jouissance 17, 105–6, 108–9; objection of 70; position of 108; as *semblant* 119; as signifier 14, 106, 107
phantasy 8, 95, 111
phenomenology 12, 122
phonation 89–90
pleasure principle 95
Pléiade (Aubert) 80
polysemy 22
polysignifyingness 78
Portrait of the Artist as a Young Man, A (Joyce): as autobiography 3, 25–6, 35, 41, 44, 51, 59; enigma in 88, 91; epiphanisation in 84; language of 33, 60; last words of 51, 71; praxis 102–4; readability of 77
psychoanalysis: aiming at the Real 95, 112; bypassing Name-of-the-Father 101–2, 112; and the desire for awakening 96; as dupe of the Father 97; use of equivocation in 74–5, 78; free association in 1, 2, 16, 17, 86; and Freud's novel 7–10; as hermeneutics 5; and jouissance 75, 87, 96, 108; of Joyce 3, 98; Lacan's reinvention of 2, 16, 112, 120, 123; use of language 18, 35, 61, 96, 112–14; literature and 1, 5; meaning in 75; transference in 112
psychoanalysts: desire of 112; end of 3; interest in Joyce 4, 55, 62, 76–7, 93, 98; interest in meaning 73–4; and jouissance 108; knowledge of 3; use of language by 83; vs. literary critics 76–7; and the Real 112, 125; responsibility of 125
psychosis 16, 40, 43, 51, 64, 83, 105, 109, 111, 118; use of equivocation in 74
push-to-the-woman symptom 59, 64, 118

quiddity 92
quilting points 16

Radiophonie (Lacan) 114, 118
rapport, sexual *see* sexual rapport
Rat Man 12

readymades 84
Real: as aim of psychoanalysis 95, 112, 120; and the *Bedeutung* of the phallus 107; beyond norms 114–23; defence against 95, 112; disconnect from the Imaginary 8, 16, 17, 43; existential 121; of jouissance 2, 17, 19, 43, 58, 95, 96, 98, 112, 124; of *lalangue* 19; of the letter 2, 76, 91; literature of 31, 86; names of the Reals 123–5; as one of the three consistencies 2, 14, 16, 55, 96, 101, 105; outside meaning 24; outside of narrative 124; and psychoanalysis 95; relationship with the Symbolic 17, 35, 40, 45, 53, 63, 68, 69, 73, 79, 86, 91, 106, 108; relationship with the unconscious 2, 60, 107, 108; as responsibility of the psychoanalyst 125; signifiers of 17, 78, 81, 83, 85; and the sinthome 41; as source of symptom 10, 122, 125; stories about 8; unknotting from 53, 55; *see also* Borromean knot; reality
reality 41, 61, 64, 71–2, 95, 96, 98, 118, 123; of fathers 34; psychic 14; sexual 14, 106; social 68; subjective 31; *see also* Real
Resnais, Alain 82
Rome: Freud's love of 26, 27, 29, 30; Joyce's aversion to 26–30
Roussel, Raymond 76
R.S.I. (Real, Symbolic, Imaginary) Seminar 2, 13, 14, 15–18, 45, 47, 63, 74, 121
RUCS (Real Unconscious) 2, 60, 108
Russell, Bertrand 9, 92, 122, 199

Sainte-Anne Hospital 3, 49, 83
savoir-faire 85, 101, 102–3, 104, 114; *see also* know-how
Schechner, Mark 4
schizophrenia 79
Schreber case 15, 41, 42, 45, 48, 58, 64, 105, 106, 114, 118
self, love of 57; *see also* narcissism
Seminar IV: La relation d'objet 65, 117, 118
Seminar V: Les formations de l'inconscient 118
Seminar X: L'angoisse (Anxiety) 9, 47

Seminar XI: Les quatre concepts fondamentaux 2
Seminar XIV: La logique du fantasme 8, 98
Seminar XVIII: D'un discours qui ne serait pas du semblant 92
Seminar XX: Encore 20, 84, 107, 112
Seminar XXI: Les non-dupes errent 18, 47, 102
Seminar XXII: R.S.I. (Real, Symbolic, Imaginary) 2, 13, 14, 15–18, 45, 47, 63, 74, 121
Seminar XXIII: Le sinthome 1, 2–3, 4, 7, 14, 21–2, 34, 39–40, 46, 73, 74, 85, 101, 102, 111, 113, 121; differing versions of first lessons 21–2
sex ratio 109, 122
sexual constitution 121
sexuality *see* heterosexuality; homosexuality
sexual norms 118
sexual rapport 65, 68, 69, 70, 111, 118–19, 120; *see also* sexual relationships
sexual relationships 10–12, 13, 65, 66, 107, 109; *see also* sexual rapport
sexual revolution 119
sexual symptom 120
sexuation 14, 64, 115, 118, 122
sinthome 18, 43, 93, 105; being 36; defined 14; dupe of 96; ego- 105; father as 14–15, 16, 17–18, 40, 105; heretical 21; Joyce fashioning 102; -name 108; naming 43; and the Real 41; rule 23–4; -saying 24; as saying 17–18; *saying-* 98, 104, 125; stepladder 59, 60; substantialisation of 73, 101, 108; substitution 91; as *suppléance* 42, 52; supplementation 71, 113, 119; *see also Seminar XXIII: Le sinthome*
sinthome-Père 40; *see also père-sinthome*
socialism 30–1
Sollers, Philippe 39
somatology 59
speech, operation of 104–10
Stephen Hero (Joyce) 25, 33, 41, 46, 60, 75, 77, 91, 103; enigma in 88
stepladder 92–3
stepladder-*sinthome* 59, 60
subjective attribution 83
subjective constitution 53, 120, 121, 123
sublimation 91; narcissistic 58

Summa Theologica (Thomas Aquinas) 3, 22
suppléance 40–2, 52
supplementation 112, 113, 119, 121, 122; through art 104–10
Symbolic: connection with Imaginary 8, 16, 17, 40, 41–2, 58, 59–60, 73, 76; connection with the Real 17, 35, 53, 63, 68, 69, 73, 79, 86, 91, 105, 106, 108, 121, 122; exemption of Joyce's texts from 86; and the generation of meaning 86; in Joyce's texts 86, 91; and the Oedipus complex 64; as one of three consistencies 2, 14, 104, 105; Other of 112, 120; of signifiers 24; unknotting from 53, 55; *see also* Borromean knot
symptome-père 15
symptom partners 13, 15, 59
symtomatology 39, 43, 59, 66, 98

Télévision (Lacan) 17, 119
Thanatos 16
Thomas Aquinas (saint) 3, 22, 80, 84, 94
Thom's Dictionary 22
Three Essays on the Theory of Sexuality (Freud) 11
Totem and Taboo (Freud) 9, 115
transference 2, 4, 98, 112
trauma 17; metaphor of 13, 17; repetition of 43

truth 25, 41, 91; and fiction 8–9; foreclosure of 17; and logic 34–6; questioning 21; *see also* Real

Ulysses (Joyce) 1, 22, 36, 51–2, 76, 77, 78–9
unconscious 2; denial of 68; Freudian 112; Freud's interest in 95; hypothesis of 112; Joyce's denial of 75, 103; learning to read 61–2; and making love 69; *motérialité of* 83; real (RUCS) 2, 60, 108; and sexual relations 13; as a spoken language 109; status of 61–2; work of 5
unreadables 76; letters 77–80
Urverdrängung 42–3

verbal games 22–4
Villanelle of the Temptress, The (Joyce) 82
virility 27, 54, 117

White, Terence Gervais 74
women: erotic use of body by 58; and the sex strike 115; as symptom 67–8, 119
word play 22–4, 76, 103
word trade 62
writer's block 3
written work, function of 3